THE FOUR GIVES OF FORGIVENESS

DEVELOPING A PREEMPTIVE MINDSET TOWARD FORGIVENESS

TODD WHALEY

KACY WHALEY-GREEN

CONTENTS

A Note From Kacy

Assisting with this book is a journey for me because I have no preconceived idea or format on how to write a book. I am, in fact, simply trusting it to come together. Language has always been my passion. I hold a core belief that most of our turmoil comes from an inability to communicate with complete honesty. Most of us maneuver around learned behaviors, teachings, beliefs, negative experiences, intellectual confines, and the fear of being ridiculed. But how else should we communicate except from the place of complete vulnerability? So, I lay bare before You, Elohim. I trust that in doing so, I can be utterly empty for Your Spirit to move freely. Elohim, the Most High Creator who gives all gifts and forges all talent; You who is the breath of all language, be my guide.

Kacy

The Work of Profession

F irst off, I would like to share how this study on forgiveness came to be. I am a licensed massage therapist who specializes in the modalities of structural bodywork. It is a profession that allows me to do the things I most enjoy, helping others and sharing my faith in the sovereign authority of Jesus Christ.

I love people, I love Jesus, and I have a deep respect and appreciation for the ability to connect those two loves daily. I take my responsibilities very seriously. I spend a great deal of time studying in my profession of therapy and my profession of faith. So, when I am providing hands-on therapy sessions with a patient, I am in constant submitted prayer, opening myself up to see the bigger picture, seeking the core problem. Core problems are rarely apparent as surface pain and suffering always have a root. My goal is to identify the origin and work from that position.

I have a female client in her sixties who came to me regularly for a series of treatments. We identified some issues, and with consistent work, she progressed perfectly. I could not have asked for better success from therapy. Out of the blue, and for no reason we could explain, she digressed. Her pain came back with all of the old issues present. We discussed it to no avail, each of us puzzled by the sudden change. One day as I was working on her, I felt moved to inquire deeper into her personal life so I asked if she had experienced any significant life changes. She became highly emotional as she began to tell me how both of her parents had passed away, and in the process of managing the estate, she became aware of sibling conflict.

This conflict had existed for some time, however, she had never been made aware of the issue. She had an older brother and two younger siblings, and when her parents died, what she thought she had as a family disintegrated. She learned that her two younger siblings hated her and her older brother, thus began great controversy over the estate. The property was divided evenly and appraised. The contention worsened when the two younger siblings wanted to sell their portion of the estate and my patient and her brother were financially able to purchase this portion and offered to do so. The younger siblings told them they would only sell their share of the property if she and the older brother would pay double the appraised value. Can you imagine the pain and suffering heaped onto my patient? She was experiencing deep grief, anger, and resentment. She told me she didn't know what to do about it. I continued working with her while listening to her story offering the best advice I know, "You need to forgive them." Of course, she already knew that, but emotional and physical pain almost always cloud our view. As we talked, I suggested she speak with her pastor about this, knowing he could help her through this process. I also gave her scripture to aid in studying the biblical call for forgiveness.

A couple of weeks later, she returned, and the first thing she said to me was this: "Okay, Mr. Preacher Man, I need some help." I asked her to continue. She explained that she spoke with her minister, read the scriptures I gave her and the scriptures he gave her. She says, "I understand the importance of forgiveness. You tell me I need to forgive, my pastor tells me I need to forgive, and Jesus tells me." "Paul tells me, and there are stories that explain the value of forgiving, but I have one problem with it." "No one tells me how." "The Bible does not explain how." She goes on to say that forgiveness is an obscure, ambiguous concept. She knew it was there, she knew it was valuable, but she didn't know how to attain it. She described it as "trying to grasp smoke." I explained to her, of course, the answer is there because our God is not an author of confusion and doesn't interact with us from ambiguous concepts. So, she asked me to research it and bring my findings back to her. So, this short mission to help my patient became a six-month endeavor. And, as in so many cases, what I thought I was doing to help her, actually helped me.

I explored the Bible in a way I had never studied before by taking a deep, contemplative approach. I was looking for a practical, step-by-step, systematic avenue for forgiveness. What I discovered was a four-step course of action outlined in the Bible. There is no single chapter, verse, or story that offers information on forgiveness. It is, in fact, the entire foundation and underlying theme of the ministry of Jesus Christ. Here's the realistic, step by step pattern I discovered:

The Four Gives of Forgiveness

1. Give up our view of the world and take on Christ's view of the world.
2. Give Satan the finger.
3. Give ourselves and all our hurt over to God.
4. Give the people who hurt us over to God.

The bedrock of our relationship with God is based upon forgiveness, which is outlined from Genesis to resurrection Sunday. It begins in The Garden and ends with the completed work of the Cross. Because it came to me in four steps, I have titled the book The Four Gives of Forgiveness.

God has blessed me in this study, in the classes forged from it, and in preparing this book. I trust you will come away forever changed, forever free.

-Todd

ALIGNING OUR
THOUGHTS

S ometimes when studying ideas and thoughts from another viewpoint, there arises a breakdown in communication. We are all unique beings with valuable, diverse understandings. I want to lay out a few things that often become controversial. Not to assert an opinion or try and sway your perspectives, but to offer a point of reference for some ideas and language personalities that could prevent someone from understanding the intent of the message. This happens often and can hinder communication. I trust the Holy Spirit to guide me in delivering this heartfelt revelation, and equally, I trust Him to give you the insight and understanding you are seeking.

DEFINITIONS

- The word "sin" comes from the Greek word "hamartia," which means: to miss the mark or to err.

- Self or Identity: 1) Original Creation: Spiritual, Eternal, Soul, Sacred, etc. 2) Fallen Man: Flesh, carnal, primitive, limited logic, temporal
- Forgiveness: Not repaying wrong with wrong and not repaying eye for an eye. Allowing full judgment and justice to rest in God's hands and God alone. Not paying back or paying forward any wrongs imposed upon you. Not projecting the wrong that was done to you onto others.
- Holy Spirit: Advocate; Comforter; Counselor; Witness; Defender; Paraclete
- The Holy Spirit is a Warrior leading us through the journey of Spiritual Warfare. This is important because when we make a conscious choice to break free from the entanglement of unforgiveness, the enemy is coming in strong!

THE FIRST GIVE OF FORGIVENESS

GIVE UP OUR VIEW OF THE WORLD TO TAKE ON CHRIST'S VIEW OF THE WORLD

T his chapter is the foundation of the book because forgiveness is not just a decision we make casually. It is, in fact, a radical act of obedience and one that requires total selflessness. Forgiveness is only successful when that surrender is given to God. Even the choice, the decision to surrender must be given to God lest we pridefully take it upon ourselves. One thing that is vital to remember as we walk through this study: everything we do is for God.

Everything we do is to make us more "Christ-like." The enemy wants all the attention and has a unique way of bearing it into us and our prideful nature. He wants it to be "all about me all the time." He will rob us of the joy and peace that come from forgiving and manipulate us into co-dependency or some other defunct personality trait that keeps us trying to control everything and keeps us from experiencing the love of God. So, the first thing we need to clear up is this: Forgiveness is a radical act of obedience, a call to surrender ourselves more to Christ.

Forgiveness is never about the other person; it is always about oneself. If by forgiving someone we are trying to gain control over them or manipulate the situation to strengthen our ego or gain control, then we are missing the mark. Forgiveness is a lesson in complete humility, where we bring ourselves under the trusting authority of God. It requires a surrender that we've never known before. Sometimes we create a false humility and go through the motions because we don't want to surrender. We still want access to controlling the relationships in our life. But honest, life-changing, holy forgiveness will require us to make this statement of faith (or a similar statement as the Holy Spirit guides our words):

"God, I cannot and do not know what is best for me. I trust you completely with the people and the relationships in my life. I want to be totally free, totally yours and none other. By choosing to forgive the people who have harmed me, I accept the necessary responsibility required for surrender. Please forgive me for the ways I have failed and the mess I have made in trying to manipulate situations to go in my favor. Forgive me for trying to control outcomes. Thank you for showing me the weakness in my own logic. I trust You completely, to know the people who do and do not belong in my life. I forgive those who have hurt me, and I ask you to take control of those relationships. I no longer want to control others or be controlled by them. I surrender."

This is important because it is a sign we are laying down

our ego so we can pick up the Spirit. There's a battle taking place day and night, and that's the battle for our minds. We feel torn because we have two identities; Ego & Spirit. This book will deal with the simultaneous act of humbly surrendering the Ego logic while forging a strong, steadfast spirit. Ego strength has no foundation in eternal reality. It is illusory frailty rooted in self-righteousness. Spiritual strength is eternal. It is the solid foundation of the only reality that matters: eternity. Keep this in mind when you feel "strength" rise up in you. What is that "strength" grounded in? Resentment, irritation, offense, cynicism, etc. are all fruits of the Ego (flesh). There is no life there. It is the fruit of self-righteousness.

In contrast, how does the Bible describe the fruit of the Spirit?

> *22 But the fruit of the Spirit is love, joy, peace, forbearance, kindness, goodness, faithfulness, 23 gentleness, and self-control. Against such things, there is no law.*

— GALATIANS 5:22-23

The only way we can manage this is to be willing to allow God to show us His perspective. When we are willing to surrender our rightness, our knowledge, and our offenses to God, we are allowing Him to shift our perspectives. He will give us a new mind and a new heart rooted in the only reality that matters: eternity.

> ^{26} *I will give you a new heart and put a new*
> *spirit in you; I will remove from you your*
> *heart of stone and give you a heart of*
> *flesh.*
>
> — EZEKIEL 36:26

GIVING IN FOR THE WIN

Give up my view of the world, to take on Christ's view of the world. This literally means giving up my reality, or my perceived reality so I can dwell in the reality Christ established for me, which is the Kingdom of Heaven. This is especially important because we, as Christians, are committed to emulating Christ. A lot of what we hear coming from pulpits and classrooms are teachings focused on behavior modification. As a parent and teacher, I am guilty of this. The question we have to ask ourselves is this: Are we trying to "act" (behave) like Christ or, are we striving to actually "be" (indwelling) like Christ? By focusing on behavior modification, we will always be in a state of acting. Why? Because all the focus is still on the carnal self, the ego, or our own logic and ability.

The problem with this is our logic is skewed. Some of us are so strong-minded and strong-willed, we can actually walk out this life in our own strength and find some measure of success, but there is no freedom in that. We are still bound to the same old logic and false identities that have created our problems in the first place. We may be determined, but we won't be free, and joy will be fleeting if we even experience it at all. But if we focus on the indwelling spirit of Christ, our true, created Holy nature, then our behavior will follow, and it won't be an act.

Let's think of it this way. When you see successful people, you want to know more about them. You not only want to know what they have done to be successful you also want a deeper understanding of the knowledge and wisdom that lead to their success. Ultimately, you want to know how they think. So many of us try to act like Jesus without trying to better understand His thought process. We focus too much on behavior modification without having any real mind and heart revelation. Thus, hindering any lasting transformation. The formula goes something like this: We need a mind revelation that will morph into a heart transformation, which will then organically lead to behavior modification. If your goal is total freedom from living your life based on a false identity, it is counterproductive if not impossible to rearrange, or more especially reverse these steps and have any positive lasting change take place.

How do I learn to see the world as Christ sees the world? Here is a really cool verse to start with:

> *39 Jesus said, "For judgment I have come into this world, so that the blind will see and those who see will become blind."*
>
> — JOHN 9:39

What Jesus is saying here is that He came to blind us, because we do not see things the way He sees them. That means all of us, not just "those other people." We all need a heart and mind check when it comes to the Nature of God and the reality of His Omnipotence. Jesus is saying unless we are seeking Him with all our heart, we will only be able to see ourselves and others through the eyes of the flesh (Ego) and we will have no spiritual insight. The carnal eyes can only see guilt and shame, but Jesus doesn't see that. I'm not saying He is not aware of it, but He knows who we really are. He doesn't view the world from the position of the Ego, and although He completely fulfilled the Law, not even Jesus walked in self-righteousness. He knows, who created us and why. Everything we see is in reference to good and evil. He sees from Omnipotence, beyond the cursed knowledge we gained from The Tree of The Knowledge Good & Evil. He sees what the Father sees. Let's revisit that passage on Spiritual Blindness:

> [35] *Jesus heard that they had thrown him out, and when he found him, he said, "Do you believe in the Son of Man?"*
> [36] *"Who is he, sir?" the man asked. "Tell me so that I may believe in him."*
> [37] *Jesus said, "You have now seen him; in fact, he is the one speaking with you."*
> [38] *Then the man said, "Lord, I believe," and he worshipped him.*
> [39] *Jesus said, "For judgment I have come into this world, so that the blind will see and those who see will become blind."*

> [40] *Some Pharisees who were with him heard*
> *him say this and asked, "What? Are we*
> *blind too?"*
> [41] *Jesus said, "If you were blind, you would*
> *not be guilty of sin; but now that you*
> *claim you can see, your guilt remains.*
>
> — JOHN 9:35-41

He is saying unless we become blind to our own perspectives, our own judgments, and our own carnal logic, (no matter how knowledgeable or well-studied we are) we will never be free from the guilt and shame that comes from constantly focusing on sinful behavior. We will see ourselves from the unstable, unreliable false identity of the flesh and therefore we will continue to live life from false beliefs formed from that carnal identity. We will continue down the path of guilt, shame, and self-righteousness and we will take a lot of people with us. We will never be whole and know the freedom that comes with allowing Christ to blind us and then reveal to us our true identity. He offers us TOTAL freedom through forgiveness.

Why can't we see it? We keep saying how unworthy we are, how bad we are, how sinful we are, how guilty, guilty, guilty, and filled with shame we are. We have the advantage of living life this side of The Cross, and we are still screaming the false narrative that Satan assigned us at the fall of Eden. If we cannot see our own Holy nature, we will never be able to see it in others. It must be a slap in the face of Jesus when we won't accept Grace. It's like saying, "We appreciate what you did on the Cross and Resurrecting and all that, but we really don't deserve it so we're just going to talk about sin a whole lot more and try to work through it and maybe if we try really hard, we can clean up our act and come back to you once we are holier."

Can you see how absurd it is to think you can approach The Finished Work of Christ with that kind of mindset? It is a self-righteous, false humility? We cannot shame ourselves into The Kingdom, it does not work that way. When we only see and point out the sins of others, we are speaking to and through the wrong identity. We are validating that we have no idea who we really are because we have no idea who Jesus really is. We have never allowed ourselves to be forgiven, (or have never admitted we need forgiving). We are still wallowing in shame and self-righteousness. We either accept we will never be good enough, or we believe we will enter the Kingdom of Heaven because we have followed all the rules, gained the right understandings, done all the good things, never committed any of the "big" sins. This way of thinking doesn't provide the surrender needed to be in a position of acceptance. It doesn't work because all focus is on our behavior, not our "being." Why would anyone want to listen to that kind of logic? It's a lie that binds us to a false identity, there is no freedom in it. Holiness=Humility and not the false kind.

There is no better example of that than the perfect being of Christ nailed to the Cross. When we allow ourselves to see through the eyes of Christ, we will not only be able to see our need for forgiveness, we will be able to accept it, and THAT is when everything will begin to change. We cannot give something we do not have. This is a simultaneous act of receiving and giving. When we ask God to help us forgive those who have wronged us, we are opening ourselves up for God to reveal the absurdity in our very basic, skewed (limited) human logic. By revealing Himself to us and through us as our authentic identity and true nature, God is shining a light on the fleshly, carnal mind of self-serving preservation. He's not shaming us when He does this. He is revealing our TRUE, Kingdom of Heaven, eternal identity. Receiving the Love of God through forgiveness will bring a level of wholeness and freedom, we won't have to try to forgive and love others. It will be a natural, organic response. We will fall in love with others as Christ commanded:

> [34] *"A new command I give you: Love one another. As I have loved you, so you must love one another.*
>
> — JOHN 13:34

This takes the Golden Rule to another whole level. Christ isn't saying. "Do unto others as you would have them do unto you." Although this is a good standard, we don't all treat ourselves with loving-kindness. We aren't just dealing with one another from the false, self-righteous identity of Ego, we are actually egotistically dealing with ourselves. So, Christ gave us an all-new commandment, which completely takes the focus off of ourselves and points us to God. Again, in John 15: [9] "As the Father has loved me, so have I loved you. Now remain in my love. [10] If you keep my commands, you will remain in my love, just as I have kept my Father's commands and remain in his love. [11] I have told you this so that my joy may be in you and that your joy may be complete. [12] My command is this: Love each other as I have loved you.

In order for us to love others, we must allow the love of God upon ourselves. Anything other than the love of God is a lie. Read that again: ANYTHING other than the love of God is a LIE. ANYTHING OTHER THAN THE LOVE OF GOD IS A LIE. Now measure your language, your actions, your projections, etc up against THAT LOVE, and if you are confused about what that love looks like, read and re-read 1 Corinthians 13 until your heart explodes. THAT is what love is and Jesus Christ exemplified it perfectly in His completed ministry. COMPLETED, meaning death and resurrection.

PARADIGM SHIFT

The Ministry of Reconciliation

> *From now on, then, we do not know anyone from a worldly perspective. Even if we have known Christ from a worldly perspective, yet now we no longer know him in this way.* ***17*** *Therefore, if anyone is in Christ, he is a new creation; the old has passed away, and see, the new has come!* ***18*** *Everything is from God, who has reconciled us to himself through Christ and has given us the ministry of reconciliation.* ***19*** *That is, in Christ, God was reconciling the world to himself,*

> *not counting their trespasses against*
> *them, and he has committed the message*
> *of reconciliation to us.*
> **20** *Therefore, we are ambassadors for Christ,*
> *since God is making his appeal through*
> *us. We plead on Christ's behalf, "Be*
> *reconciled to God." **21** He made the one*
> *who did not know sin to be sin for us, so*
> *that in him we might become the right-*
> *eousness of God.*

— 2 CORINTHIANS 5:16-21 (CSB)

When Jesus looks at the world, He sees a total battlefield. He sees the battle of flesh and spirit. Satan has assigned us carnal identity, and Christ has revealed (not just talked about it but showed us) the truth about who we really are. This is our only real battle. It's the root of all dysfunction: Spiritual vs. Carnal (flesh).

Omnipotence vs. Illusion. Omnipotence/Spirit is eternal. Illusion/Flesh is temporal. So when Jesus says, "be in the world but not of the world," he is essentially saying anything that is material, fleshly, etc. is an illusion. It is temporal; it will eventually die. Anything you can see, taste, smell, or touch is an illusion... it is not real. Your holiness is real, your divinity is real...your original design is real. Your Spirit is not an illusion it is eternal, it is your true identity. And when we learn to maneuver life from this perspective, we can enter the Kingdom of Heaven right here, right now. The only thing that is real here on Earth is our love for one another. Love is the ONLY thing that can survive in eternity. Jesus walked this out. Jesus sees the difference between the illusory man and the spiritual man; there are many references to this in the Bible.

I direct your attention to the following verses:

> *"The lord is my shepherd I shall not want,"*
> *implies no fear, no desire, nothing lack-*
> *ing. Meaning ALL of our needs covered.*
> *When the flesh comes under the order of*
> *the Spirit we will want for NOTH-*
> *ING.... NO desire. We will be filled and*
> *overflowing.*

— PSALM 23:1

> *"I came to give you life abundantly." In the*
> *Greek, this means an ever-flowing, inex-*
> *haustible source that fills a container in*
> *constant overflow.*

— JOHN 10:10

"My God will supply every need according to His riches." Every means every.... All means all. There are no arbitrary concepts in the Bible. According to His riches means just what it says. It does not mean according to your hard labor, your logic, your concepts, or your beliefs. It is strictly by His standard, His measure, His ability, and His love for us...period. By maintaining our focus on Him and Him alone, our work, logic, and our ability will come under the Spirit, which is our original design. From that place, that

Holy position of surrender, we will see things through His eyes. Our logic will become a spiritual source grounded in our focus on Him and Him alone, and all His goodness will overflow into our lives as a never-ending well of abundance.

> *"Therefore I tell you, DO NOT WORRY,*
>   *about your life, what you will eat or*
>   *drink; or about your body, what you will*
>   *wear. Is not life more than food and*
>   *body more than clothes?"*
>
> — MATTHEW 6:25

Again, DO NOT WORRY, DO NOT BE CONCERNED. But, what? Instead of worry and concern what are we to do? "Seek first the Kingdom of God and ALL these things will be added." All means all... and with our focus on Kingdom realities it does not mean OUR all, it means GOD'S all. It is a kind of "all" that we can't even imagine. His abundance is not dependent upon our economy, not influenced by our political structure or laws. His source is beyond human logic, beyond our physical and mental ability. He does not need our education, our skill, our plan, or our well-played hand. He does not need our rightness or our goodness, He is good enough. Surrender is the only option here. His abundance is a river, flowing from an endless, inexhaustible source, seeking an empty vessel (surrendered souls) to fill and to continue filling with an abundance as we have never seen. All we need to do is keep our focus on that promise. He loves us, and His love for us fulfilled in His promises to us is the only thing that ever matters. What is this promise? "ALL these things will be added unto to you." That is Kingdom living, that is a Kingdom reality. Let's give up the illusion, the temporal view, and stand at the edge of quantum realities. HEAVEN ON EARTH!

Trusting His Promises

> The Lord said to Moses, "Send some men to explore the land of Canaan, which I am giving to the Israelites. From each ancestral tribe send one of its leaders."
>
> — Numbers 13:2

What is God saying here? Send out these twelve men to explore "*that which I am giving to you*." "Meaning it has been done, has been given. That is a promise. But what happened? Ten came back saying, "The land is just as God promised, it flows with milk and honey,

BUT...

Anytime we encounter God, anytime He reveals His promises to us we should be cautious about adding a "but":

- *"but the people there are powerful, and the cities are fortified and very large."*
- *"but we seem like grasshoppers in our own eyes and we looked the same to them."*
- *"but we cannot attack these people, they are stronger than us."*

Now, in contrast to those ten men, what did the other two have to say? The two men who trusted God believed Him. They could clearly see the world from God's perspective. Caleb said, "We should go and take possession of the land, for WE CAN CERTAINLY DO IT." Caleb & Joshua were not confused. They saw exactly what the others had seen, but their viewpoint was different. They saw everything God had promised. They were in the world but not of the world; walking, breathing, and operating from the perfect place of never-ending, inexhaustible, overflowing, omnipotent abundance.

Were the previous reports accurate? From their perspectives, sure they were. Did the others lie or bring back a false report? No... they told exactly what they saw. The problem here is that they did not believe in God's word. Their logic (ego) was still wrapped around the temporal world, the illusion...so much so, that they could not see through God's eyes. They completely lost sight of His omnipotence. They no longer relied upon Him, they relied upon their own ability thus limiting if not cutting themselves off from His abundant source. This was their birthright. It had been prophesied and promised. In less than 24 hours, ten men using primitive logic, tainted with doubt and fear presented an illusory (limited) report and turned two million people against God. They completely threw a shadow over the two faithful followers, who knew God, knew He was trustworthy, and stood firm on His love for them. What the ten others saw as an insurmountable obstacle, Caleb and Joshua saw as bread. When the others said, "We cannot do this," Caleb and Joshua said... "Let's go eat."

Is this not the same attitude David had when he stood before Goliath? David could not afford to rely on the illusory, worldly realities. Facts of the flesh rarely, if ever align with the promises of God. The fleshly logic (ego) serves a purpose, but only when it is aligned underneath the Spirit. It is interested in one thing only, self-preservation at all costs. It is the most primitive logic of instinct that binds us to this illusion/temporal world. Learning the difference in the nature of the two helps us understand our divisiveness and why we cannot seem to reconcile ourselves with a Kingdom mindset. We have to learn to rely solely upon God's love for us fulfilled in His promises to us. How else will we ever be able to see the world and the people of the world through His eyes? How will we ever be able to see ourselves through His eyes? And the best part of this is, that as His promises are continually fulfilled, as our cup runs over, His faithfulness becomes tangible, manifested realities. You've heard the saying, "I have to see it to believe it." That is not biblical, that's a lie. If we are going to walk out the Kingdom of Heaven, which is our birthright, our established reality, we will have to lay down that false logic.

The reality of God is: "You have to believe it to see it." I'm not saying that troubles of the world don't exist, I'm just saying there is another reality we can walk in, but we cannot do that while constantly feeding the primitive, logical mindset trapped in the flesh. There was evidence presented to the Israelites, and they made a decision based on their fleshly logic. In doing so, they missed out on the promises of God. They saw what they saw, and because of that, they suffered the result of their unbelief. God says, "You have to believe it to see it." After the non-believing generation died away, the Benjamin generation went in. When they approached the Amalekites, they just yelled at them and the giants fell dead. Jericho is another example of this; they never raised weaponry. They just did exactly as God ordered. Strength through humility.

Another reminder of the authority that rises up when we operate with solid belief, is in the Garden of Gethsemane. When the Roman soldiers asked, "Which of you is Jesus." Jesus spoke saying, "I AM," and they all fell on their faces. If we accept the truth, "As He is, so are we," (1 John 4:17), why do we not walk with that authority? Is it unbelief? Do we believe what we say? Have we become comfortable with our doctrine, or are we cultivating a relationship with Christ, that allows us to wrestle unbelief? It all boils down to building a solid faith in Christ, so we can truly learn to surrender and FULLY TRUST HIS WILL FOR OUR LIVES. This sure removes a lot of unnecessary labor, stress, worry, and fear. The Bible is filled with over 7000 promises God made specifically to mankind. Surely, among them, we can find solid ground on which to stand in most any situation life brings.

BELIEVE IT TO SEE IT

There is not one account in The Bible where God says He is going to give us strength and courage to deal with our affliction. He will if we ask for that, but we need to shift our focus from our affliction to God. Every time, Jesus says that God is going to be glorified in sickness, it always ends in complete healing.... every time!!!!!! One of Satan's greatest weapons is religion. We take scripture, especially the most obscure scripture, and interpret it to accommodate our lack of faith. That's religion. Instead of reading and studying the Word to grow closer to God and increase our faith, we read to secure our own logic. We try to cram the Word of God into our already established beliefs about Him. We don't really believe in Him.... we believe in our beliefs about Him. This is foolish. It is like building a house on sinking sand, and goes directly against his instruction for us in Proverbs:

> *5 Trust in the Lord with all your heart,*
> *And lean not on your own understanding;*
> *6 In all your ways acknowledge Him,*
> *And He shall direct your paths.*
>
> — PROVERBS 3:5-6 NKJV

Surrendering our beliefs to God and learning to lean on Him and Him alone is the beginning of seeing through His eyes.

THE KNOWLEDGE OF GOOD AND EVIL

Television, radio, internet, etc. are also inexhaustible, abundant, and overflowing sources of information.....***confusion.*** 24 hours a day, 7 days a week we are fed viable facts in every form, most of which incite fear, anxiety, frustration, division, and an abundance of self-righteousness. We then allow those facts to enter our minds and direct our flesh. We are blasted with sarcasm, satire, poetry, artwork, etc... .all free thought expressions based upon facts, facts, facts that spread lies, lies, lies, disguised as truth, about any subject you can imagine. We all want to be in "the know." How reliable is any of this information and where is your focus when participating in it?

Remember this: ***The source of original sin is the knowledge of good and evil.*** I am so guilty of this, and if you are reading this book you are likely in the same position. When we start to feel anxious, indignant, afraid, angry, and a whole psych-storm of negative emotions we need to ask one thing. Where is our focus? If we are feeling divisiveness, we are not in alignment with God... We are not in alignment with the source...we are not walking in a Kingdom reality. What does God say? Be anxious for nothing.... Do not worry.... Be not afraid.... I am with you.... I have you in the palm of my hand... I will never leave you.

Here is the key, and remember this: ***Facts of the flesh will rarely, if ever, line up with God's promises.*** If we are viewing the world from any perspective or position other than a place of total security in God's love for us, then we will always be teetering in the instabilities that come with ego-consciousness. We will constantly battle the dual extremes of the flesh... either self-pity, self-loathing, uncertainty, etc . or the opposite extreme of contrite, arrogance, melodramatic, pretentious, phony, etc. This all still stems from a "self" disconnected from its original creator and source of love. Remember: Opposite sides of the coin, are still of the same coin. ALL our relationships will be skewed when we operate from the phony, illusory mindset of the flesh.

If we can't see ourselves through God's eyes, how can we ever see the world and others through His eyes? If we can't see our own Holiness as our original identity, we will be forever lost in the illusion of this world and the false identities assigned by the enemy. We will never be good enough, pretty enough, strong enough, smart enough and we will be forever trapped in the confusion that is so apparent in the illusory world of "media."

At some point, we have to realize that confusion only comes with divisiveness. If we have not reconciled ourselves to the full truth of God's love for us, then we have failed to clearly understand the finished work of the Cross of Jesus Christ. If we are still trying to "work through" our sin, or if we believe in anything other than God's love for us as fulfilled in His promises to us, we are still seeing ourselves and the world through the eyes of our ego. Jesus offers total freedom from the world. Don't settle for less than EVERYTHING for which He died to give YOU.

EGO AND THE LAW

Unless the ego is successfully brought under the Holy Spirit, we will continue to operate under the illusion of the law. The ego loves to talk about the law, because it condemns. It is like the media. It reveals an apparent truth but leaves out the most fundamental aspects of reality. It is pretentious and accusing. The law will constantly point back at the flesh bringing the focused accusation to lack, inability, and unworthiness. One thing the law cannot do is reveal our Holiness. The law cannot reveal God's love. That's why Paul says, "For the strength of sin lies in the law." The law reveals sin, not love. The law secures sin, not love.

The law will never bring freedom because it keeps all the focus on the flesh. It binds us to the flesh and keeps us in a vicious cycle of behavior modification using the same fleshly logic that created the problems in the first place. It keeps us striving for approval and worthiness when Christ already showed us that we are worth it. It keeps us from accepting His truth. It keeps us from trusting Him. It keeps us trapped in the illusion because the law is unnecessary in the Kingdom of Heaven. So many of us Christians have been measuring ourselves against laws of the flesh, and in doing so we encounter shame, jealousy, guilt, lust, manipulation, etc.

We keep the enemy at the forefront of EVERYTHING. Because of this misunderstanding, all we can see is sin, and we continue to heap condemnation upon ourselves and others. We focus more on sickness instead of wellness, more on darkness instead of holiness, more on problems than solutions.

One thing is for sure... we cannot focus on sin and God at the same time. We cannot fully receive the overflowing gift of grace while desperately hanging on to the false narrative of unworthiness. We cannot walk in the reality of the established Kingdom of Heaven by trying to be something we already are. Salvation is not by any effort of our own, and it never will be. Grace is a gift, given in love. Please don't ever allow yourself to reduce God's love to an earned wage. Grace is not cheap... it is free.

If you try to measure it through labor, you will NEVER BE ABLE TO RECEIVE IT. The law is the curse of self-righteousness. Remember the Tree of the Knowledge of Good and Evil? The Knowledge of Good is just as condemning as the Knowledge of Evil. Opposite sides of the coin are still of the same coin. Our knowledge presents problems that can only be healed in our full, willing surrender. Grace cannot be attained or achieved within the mind. It is only through surrender that we can be emptied enough to receive it.

Divisiveness begins within us long before it manifests as a fleshly reality. This is why you cannot mix Grace and Law. **What did Jesus say, "I would that you were hot or cold but not lukewarm or I will spew you from my mouth." Hot, representing His blood covering ...cold representing the stone tablets of the law.

Christ revealed our true identity so the enemy could no longer deceive us about who we are. His grave reveals clearly how much God loves us. His resurrection reveals our true identity. Both define the Finished Work of The Cross and reveal completely, His Grace. Grace is the abundant source of Kingdom realities. Grace is our inexhaustible well. Jesus is saying choose one or the other.

Receive grace and gain total freedom. When we walk with a law-based mindset, we find we can never overcome the flesh. We will not know the kind of freedom that comes with the fullness of grace until we have exhausted all effort and rest in total surrender to HIS LOVE FOR US.

The law cannot offer anything other than shame, unworthiness, and the deceit of self-righteousness. Christ fulfilled ALL LAWS, and that is where our true, eternal identity is. Grace and shame cannot exist in the same place. We know shame cannot survive in our omnipotent, Kingdom of Heaven reality. The Spirit reality can only be revealed in Grace. Grace is not freedom to sin; Grace is freedom from sin. There is *no other measure and no other way!* Consider this passage from Revelation 3:15-20 (NASB):

> [15] 'I know your deeds, that you are neither cold nor hot; I wish that you were cold or hot. [16] So because you are lukewarm, and neither hot nor cold, I will vomit you out of My mouth. [17] Because you say, "I am rich, and have become wealthy, and have no need of anything," and you do not know that you are wretched, miserable, poor, blind, and naked, [18] I advise you to buy from Me gold refined by fire so that you may become rich, and white garments so that you may clothe yourself and the shame of your nakedness will not be revealed; and eye salve to apply to your eyes so that you may see. [19] Those whom I love, I rebuke and discipline; therefore, be zealous and repent. [20] Behold, I stand at the door and knock; if anyone hears My voice and opens the door, I will come in to him and will dine with him, and he with Me.

A few years ago, I was visiting Tallahassee, Florida. It is the home of Core Institute where I attended massage school and obtained my certification. I returned all along for bodywork and to just visit the city I had come to know as a second home. While visiting, my wife Tammy and I decided to stop at Lake Ella, a sweet spot to hang out overlooking a small lake. I noticed a man tying a small dog to a park bench just outside a porta-potty. The man secured the pup, then stepped away to use the restroom. The dog seemed fine until he suddenly couldn't see his master. As soon as the man disappeared into the restroom, the dog started barking and snatching his leash. The harder he pulled the more frantic he became and it was only a minute before he was completely tangled up in his lead. He got so twisted, he was being choked by his own resistance., which then made him more frantic.

We tried to help him, but as we reached in to help, he would snap at us. He was scared, he just knew he was bound and in pain, he did not understand the source of his conflict and therefore could not receive our assistance. I really thought he might choke himself out. His master stepped out of the restroom, called the dog by name, and the pup immediately stopped struggling. He walks over, releases the lead, and untangles the dog. The man then walks away with the pup, leading him and the little guy is perfectly, tail-wagging happy.

As I observed the scene I felt a prompt from the Holy Spirit, as I often do. I paused to allow the nudge to come to fruition. I heard the familiar voice, "Todd, who and what is on your park bench?" I pondered that for a long time. The reason this is so important is that we are tied, twisted, and tethered to defining hurts throughout our lives. People, events, betrayals, humiliations, etc. are defining moments where we lost our Eden, where we lost our innocence, where we became deceived and believed a lie about ourselves. We are chained to those insults and injuries, and we are fighting, pulling, barking, arguing, and resisting help. We are running around in circles, tied and tethered to the pain, choking the life out of ourselves in our own struggle. We are doing this to ourselves, and we have no one else to blame for our behavior. BUT, if we will allow the master to give us a new name, a new identity, and a new lead when he calls us, we will know his voice and NOTHING THAT HAS EVER HAPPENED IN THE PAST OR MAY HAPPEN IN THE FUTURE WILL REMOVE US FROM HIS PROTECTIVE LEAD. We will see and know the abundant life he has for us and be able to walk in that freedom.

FACTS & LOGIC

There will always be logical evidence, which makes perfect sense in the natural world but speaks directly against the Love of God. It all boils down to one thing.... Do we actually believe all the things we say we believe? Do we believe God is real? Do we believe He loves us? Do we believe we can trust Him? Do we believe Jesus to be whom He says? Are we leaning on our doctrine, our logic, our own understandings, or are we leaning 100%, totally surrendered to the Omnipotent source that gives all life and does so in abundance? Where is our focus? Why are we still eating fruit from the forbidden tree? We need to fast the fruit of that tree FOREVER! We have the privilege of living this side of the Cross and Resurrection of Christ. Why are we still desperately seeking Knowledge from the Tree of Good and Evil? There is no freedom in that cycle and all "knowledge" from that tree leads to death. There was never any life in that knowing and there never will be. Jesus fully revealed that and through that revelation restored our innocence. We just have to believe Him. Then we will be able to see ourselves, others, and the world as God sees.

From the moment we believe a lie about ourselves and become separate from him, God is constantly revealing Himself to us to restore our sight to His truth. We are shackled to certain defining moments in our life that have pulled us away from our true nature, giving us a skewed view of ourselves and the world. This is where we experience our own "fall" from Eden. When we believe the lie presented in these heartbreaking moments, we unknowingly make agreements with these lies and adopt false identities. (This is exactly what happened to Eve). Based upon this we then shift into the frame of skewed logic and continue to develop more false beliefs. Remember the phrase "believe it to see it?" These false beliefs begin manifesting a life of darkness, all of which are formed from deceitful thinking. This is the fruit of the Tree of the Knowledge of Good and Evil. This is why we live cyclical patterns of dysfunctional lives. This is why those cycles carry on generationally. Like a ball attached to a tether, we are attached to dysfunctional beliefs. We modify our behavior, feel great about making progress only to cycle back around with the same problem.

Until we are able to see ourselves through God's eyes,

we won't be able to stand in agreement with Him. We've made agreements with darkness and don't even realize it. Once we begin to see our holiness, our own divinity, we will develop beliefs that align with the truth of the Gospel of Christ. New thought patterns will form, which allow us to detach ourselves from the pole. We will automatically begin developing whole new ideas, creating and allowing space for healthier behavior to exist and flourish. Trying to modify behavior without first changing our thinking and thought patterns is almost certain failure. There is no room for the new man to be born again with the old man still attached to the lie.

Even with the best intention and the strongest willpower, behavior modification will always be focused on the lie. The lie is that we are separated from God's love. Our behavior has nothing to do with God's ability to love us. Our behavior has only to do with our ability to receive God's love. The law, the ego, the false identities can NEVER reveal the love of God. They can only reveal the nature and behavior which is assigned by the enemy. Remember, the enemy gave us those identities, we made agreements with him, and we likely continue agreeing with him day after day. He is a liar and there is no truth in him. He uses that which is true while totally removing omnipotent truth. There is no freedom there and never will be. Believe in God's truth and revelation of His love fulfilled by Christ. Christ's facts and logic are revealed in His grace. That is the only source of total freedom.

The thing we have to realize is that forgiveness is a choice and by choosing it we invite new freedoms into our lives. For most of us, making the choice to even consider forgiveness is a radical act of obedience. By doing this, what are we saying? We are saying that we are tired of divisiveness. We no longer want to live cyclical dysfunction. We know we have skewed perspectives and beliefs.

We are saying that we trust God to be faithful in His promises. We are saying that we trust in the finished work of Christ. We are accepting His invitation to bury our burdens in baptism and to awaken into an all-new resurrected life. We are saying, "Yes," to freedom. We may or may not have had a choice in where we went off track, but the choice to return is always ours. Freedom through Grace is our birthright. Let's align ourselves with this God-promised, Christ fulfilled, OMNIPOTENT TRUTH!

QUESTIONS FOR CONTEMPLATION

1. How did Jesus view this world?
2. Did he worry about lacking anything?
3. Was he worried about competition with others?
4. Was he afraid of being hurt?
5. Was he fearful of anything?
6. How did Jesus look at mankind?
7. Was he taken advantage of?
8. Was He betrayed?
9. How did he respond, and what caused him to respond the way he did?

THE SECOND GIVE OF FORGIVENESS

GIVE SATAN THE FINGER

T his chapter will deal with seeing Satan for who he really is. Once we can identify the real enemy, it becomes easier and easier to give him the finger, meaning pointing him out in every situation where there is conflict. We begin this chapter with two main objectives:

1. Know the enemy-Ephesians 6:12
2. Know how the enemy works.-Genesis 3

One thing I know for sure, the enemy does not want us to love. He does not want us to forgive. He would prefer to maneuver his agenda in the hearts and minds of as many people as possible. He wants to own the pain thus control the actions and would use his wily tactics to destroy the hearts and minds of as many people as possible. He does this by using us as his tools thus hiding behind the face of men. But once you see him, once you experience the suffering that comes with his seeping into your life, it becomes easier and easier to point him out in every heart-breaking, soul-crushing situation.

When you're able to see him for the weak, pathetic crea-ture he is, he begins to lose power in your life and the offspring of that revelation is light. Light is the birthplace of love, and love is the foundation of forgiveness. We must allow others to work out their own path, even when that path becomes an earthquake under the ground on which we stand. But God doesn't leave us there if we cry out to him. He is our rescue.

Until we become skilled at pointing out the originator of deceit, we are unable to avoid the daggers thrown on our backs. But once we see him, once we are able to clearly define for ourselves who he actually is and how he operates, we develop discernment and with it a confidence that liter-ally shoves us onto a different road where light becomes our focus and the love of God is poured out like a balm to our continually opened wounds. Remember, the enemy loves attention.

He wants it to be "all about me all the time." While working through pain and working through suffering is valuable to honor our pain, it is vital that we not get stuck in this. It is vital that we keep choosing to see the Light of the World and be cautious to not make agreements with the deceitful one. Jesus showed us how to bury our hurt and promises to resurrect us all new. ***Just don't forget where to focus***. Call the enemy out, see him for who and what he is, ***but do not confuse the people involved for the enemy***. That is his deceitful tactic. Instead, let God do his work and rest in the absolute promise that:

If God be for you then who can be against you
    (Romans 8:31)
The Lord with fight for you if only you be
    still (Exodus 14:14)

We are tempted to seek our own revenge, make our voices heard with recompense. But how much more can God do for us when we choose His love as our refuge and hiding place? Bury yourself in Him until he drowns the bitterness and watch what emerges within you. A light so holy and a new path so clear, the world won't even be the same stomping ground you once knew, and the enemy will be left in the dust for God to deal with. The ways of this world are foolish. Freedom from it really is as simple as choosing love at all costs and forgiving yourself and others for the errors that come with humanness. And remember, God wants freedom for everyone involved.... not just you.... so LET GO!

For our struggle is not against flesh and
    blood, but against the rulers, against the
    authorities, against the powers of this
    dark world and against the spiritual
    forces of evil in the heavenly realms

Read that again and again, until you know the difference between Satan and man.

Fear is the enemy's only tool. It is at the root of evil because it is often grounded in a lie. Since there are unique connotations surrounding the word "fear," let's tackle the definition before we dive deeper into the subject.

Merriam-Webster Dictionary[1] defines fear like this:

NOUN:

~an unpleasant often strong emotion caused by antici-pation or awareness of danger

~an instance of this emotion

~a state marked by this emotion

~anxious concern

~profound reverence and awe especially toward God

~reason for alarm

VERB:

~to be afraid of: expect with alarm fear the worst

~to have reverential awe God

~archaic: frighten

~archaic: to feel fear in (oneself)

It is important that we clearly define the concept of fear as it pertains to this book, so we do not confuse the message. We have an instinctual fear that helps make us aware of the danger. This type of fear is not rooted in a lie. It is usually a reasonable caution we develop from an under-standing of the world and from experiencing the conse-quence of our actions. One example I like to use is the law of gravity. Gravity is a perfect law. I respect the absolute-ness of the law of gravity. I appreciate being able to operate safely within the law of gravity. While I am not afraid of gravity, I am keenly aware of the omnipotent authority, which governs this law... even more so when I am hiking cliffside. Respecting this law may be considered a type of fear. I understand that there is a consequence, sometimes a serious consequence if I behave in a way that I mishandle myself within the law, ie falling down a flight of stairs. This type of fear is rooted in absolute truth. Such is the same with God. We don't have to be afraid of God, but we need to fear the consequence of not remaining within the freedom of His Grace. One thing that concerns me most about some doctrines is the idea that God punishes us for making mistakes. Let me say this in a different way. God is not sitting up in heaven just waiting to whack-a-man. Sin is its own punishment. Through Grace, God offers us the ability to deepen in intimacy with Him. Through that relationship, we are made aware of His ways with a wisdom that the logical world may not easily understand. Sometimes we gain understanding through meditation and study. Sometimes we gain this understanding through suffering consequences. So, as we become keenly aware of the consequence of our mistakes, we need to be even more aware of the Grace that sets us free from our dysfunctional mindset.

Remember, the one thing the enemy does consistently? He destroys relationships. This begins with skewing our view of ourselves (which then skews our view of EVERYTHING AND EVERYONE AROUND US), forcing us into hiding and developing an unnatural fear of abandonment. This type of fear is at the root of all evil because it is rooted in a lie. This lie develops an unnatural fear of the unknown, unseen, and uncertain. We will never truly trust God from this position. We will trust our own logic and behavior, which forces us into self-centered righteousness. If the enemy can convince us to be afraid of God, he knows we will never trust God enough to surrender. We will be in a sin conscious cycle where we talk about Satan and Hell way more than we talk about the Love of God poured out on Golgotha. THAT IS EXACTLY WHAT

THE ENEMY WANTS... ALL ABOUT ME ALL THE TIME. Self-righteous people are not free. They are caught up in the knowledge of good and evil... which is a curse that can only be healed in Grace. It cannot be healed with more labor, more knowledge, more doctrine, or anything outside the free love of God. Without surrendering to the fullness of Grace, we are bound in spiritual death. That does not mean that we are not saved, Jesus secured that for us. But it means we have not entered the resting place of the Kingdom of Heaven that Jesus established here for us. Are you tempted to condemn your brethren? That isn't the same as disagreeing. We will always have disagreements as long as we have breath. It also is not the same a discerning sinful behavior.

The Holy Spirit offers us the gift of discernment but forbids us to put ourselves in the judgment seat. What I mean by condemning our brethren is: Are you tempted to see other people as the enemy? Are you so focused on sin that you forget to share the finished work of the Cross. You know the old saying, "You can't give something you don't have." If you find yourself drawn to harboring bitterness, pointing fingers, and feeling overwhelmed with the dark powers of this world, then your focus is on the wrong thing. You may be talking about grace, but you haven't come to an intimate, experiential consummation with the Love of Christ.

If you haven't jumped in the deep end head first, grace is still just a concept. You will never experience true freedom this way. And that, my dear friend, is exactly what the enemy wants. He wants you to be so afraid of being abandoned by God, that you feel like there is no way out, or that the only way out is a cyclical pattern of behavior modification. If your way of modifying behavior is by focusing on the love of God, then good for you, that is doable. But if you are trying to modify behavior while focusing on the problem, then you will never be free. Even if you find some measure of success you will likely wind up in a self-righteous pattern of struggle where the focus is all about the wrong identity. The enemy wants all the attention all the time. The enemy is sin conscious and he wants you to be too. The absolute and ONLY place the enemy cannot thrive is in the loving forgiveness of the Grace of God. Sin consciousness is a human logic that has you pointing out the wrong dude, in yourself and others. Only grace consciousness can correctly identify the enemy EVERY SINGLE TIME...and guess what, it ain't the people in the other church up the road, and it ain't the ex-.

I like using these acronyms because they help me maintain an awareness of where my focus needs to be: F.E.A.R. = False evidence appearing real and E.G.O.= Edging God out. Again, fear comes from the ego and while it instinctively serves us well when applied to truth, it will always hinder our spiritual growth when based on a lie. The moment we fall into deceitful fear we begin operating from a very skewed perception. The ego is concerned with only one thing: self-preservation at all costs. When aligned with our Holy Identity and surrendered to the Love of God, our ego takes its rightful place and we begin bearing the fruit of the Spirit. When aligned with deceitful logic, we breed resistance and our ego bears the fruit of rebellion.

KNOW HOW THE ENEMY WORKS

If we are going to be able to give the enemy the finger, then we have to examine how he works. Here is the entire Chapter 3 of Genesis. Below it, I am going to break it down in my own words. When I quote scripture, I encourage people to study for themselves. God knows exactly where we are, exactly what we are seeking and exactly how to reach us. He wants to meet us where we are, but He doesn't want to leave us there. His desire is that we would learn to meditate and study, allowing Him to renew our understanding thereby renewing our strength in Him. So, I have shown the entire chapter here, and below it is just me mansplaining. It is how it came to me as I was studying so I decided to add it to the book. BUT, I encourage you to contemplate this for yourself and see the ways it applies to you and your life.

The Temptation and Fall of Man

1 Now the serpent was more cunning than any beast of the field which the LORD God had made. And he said to the woman, "Has God indeed said, 'You shall not eat of every tree of the garden'?"

2 And the woman said to the serpent, "We may eat the fruit of the trees of the garden;

3 but of the fruit of the tree which is *in the midst of the garden, God has said, 'You*

shall not eat it, nor shall you touch it, lest
you die.' "

4 Then the serpent said to the woman, "You
will not surely die.

5 For God knows that in the day you eat of it
your eyes will be opened, and you will be
like God, knowing good and evil."

6 So when the woman saw that the
tree was good for food, that
it was pleasant to the eyes, and a tree
desirable to make one wise, she took of its
fruit and ate. She also gave to her
husband with her, and he ate.

7 Then the eyes of both of them were
opened, and they knew that
they were naked; and they sewed fig
leaves together and made themselves
coverings.

8 And they heard the sound of the LORD God
walking in the garden in the cool of the
day, and Adam and his wife hid themselves from the presence of the LORD God
among the trees of the garden.

9 Then the LORD God called to Adam and
said to him, "Where are you?"

10 So he said, "I heard Your voice in the
garden, and I was afraid because I was
naked; and I hid myself."

11 And He said, "Who told you that
you were naked? Have you eaten from

the tree of which I commanded you that
you should not eat?"

12 Then the man said, "The woman whom
You gave to be with me, she gave me of
the tree, and I ate.

13 And the LORD God said to the woman,
"What is this you have done?"

The woman said, "The serpent deceived me,
and I ate.

14 So the LORD God said to the serpent:
"Because you have done this,
you are cursed more than all cattle, And
more than every beast of the field;

on your belly you shall go, and you shall eat
dust all the days of your life.

15 And I will put enmity between you and
the woman, and between your seed
and her seed; He shall bruise your head,
and you shall bruise His heel."

16 To the woman He said: "I will greatly
multiply your sorrow and your
conception;

in pain you shall bring forth children; your
desire shall be for your husband,
and he shall rule over you."

17 Then to Adam He said, "Because you have
heeded the voice of your wife, and have
eaten from the tree of which I
commanded you, saying, 'You shall not
eat of it':

"Cursed is the ground for your sake; in toil

you shall eat of *it all the days of your life.*

18 *Both thorns and thistles it shall bring forth for you, and you shall eat the herb of the field.*

19 *In the sweat of your face you shall eat bread till you return to the ground, for out of it you were taken; for dust you* are, *and to dust you shall return."*

20 *And Adam called his wife's name Eve, because she was the mother of all living.*

21 *Also for Adam and his wife the* LORD *God made tunics of skin, and clothed them.*

22 *Then the* LORD *God said, "Behold, the man has become like one of Us, to know good and evil. And now, lest he put out his hand and take also of the tree of life, and eat, and live forever"—*

23 *therefore the* LORD *God sent him out of the garden of Eden to till the ground from which he was taken. 24So He drove out the man; and He placed cherubim at the east of the garden of Eden, and a flaming sword which turned every way, to guard the way to the tree of life.*

— GENESIS 3 NKJV

MAN-SPLAINING

Hanging out just waiting for the right time, Satan approaches Eve.

Satan: "So, how ya diggin' the Garden?"

Eve: "Oh, it's fantastic. Just look at how beautiful everything is." She looks around at the inexhaustible beauty. This freedom and peace were all she knew. She had no concept of evil and no reason whatsoever to be afraid of the snake. She knew no fear.

Satan: "So, you're completely free to roam the garden, go anywhere you want?"

Eve: "Why yes, yes we are?"

Satan: "So, do you have enough food?"

Eve: "Well, of course, we have enough food, just look around at the variety."

Satan: "Have you tried everything yet?"

Eve: "We have tended to and harvested nearly everything in this garden." "There is a fresh spring which nourishes all the plants and animals." "Our every need is met."

Satan: "Nearly?" "Did you say, nearly?" "What have you not harvested and enjoyed?"

Eve: "Well, there is this one tree we must stay away from." "The fruit looks ok, but my Dad says we need to stay away from it."

Satan: "Hmmm, do you know why he said that?"

Eve: "Dad says if we eat from that tree we will die."

Satan: "Well, are you sure he said that?" "I don't think he meant you would actually die." "Why would your dad put a tree of death in a perfect garden?" "Doesn't make sense." "Maybe you misunderstood him."

Eve: "Hmmm." "Maybe."

Satan: "I bet I know what he really meant."

Eve: "Oh yeah, what?"

Satan: "He didn't mean that you would die, he meant you wouldn't be so naïve anymore."

Eve: "Naïve?"

Satan: "Yeah, naïve.. it means not very smart."

Eve: "Are you sure?" "Why would dad do that to me?"

Satan: "If you eat of that tree you will be wise like your dad." "You will be smarter and you will know good from evil."

Eve: "What is good and evil?" "You mean if I eat that fruit I will be more like my dad?" "That would be awesome because He is a great dad." "I want to be even more like my dad." "I bet Adam would like me better then, and he might want to be more like dad too."

Satan: "Yes, you will have a broader and deeper understanding of how things are." "You will be so smart." "Just one bite, I promise you will not surely die." "Only your naivety will shift, your knowledge will increase."

Eve: "Well, you talk about my dad like you know him." "You sound really wise and I want to be wise too."

And the rest is history.

You can imagine this story however you like when applying it to all the ways you are robbed of your innocence in this life. It always begins with a lie. Going back to the actual Biblical account of Genesis 3, not my man-splained version, notice how Satan addresses Eve as "you" not "we." This is common predatory behavior. It is how innocent people are lured every day. Satan is isolating her from her true identity, away from the One who knew her fully and loved her. She continues to refer to herself as "we" until he introduces the doubt of "not enough" into her mind. Then she begins to think of herself and an "I" outside of God, Adam, and the beings of the Garden. The minute we see ourselves as anything other than the absolute perfect Love of God, we are not whole. We are divided, conflicted, and lost in confusion. And just like Eve led Adam in the same direction with the same flawed perspective using the same predatory behavior, we too lead and are led. Until we see our true Christ nature we will continue to struggle... CONSTANTLY STRUGGLE trying to be something we already are.

I was always taught the Genesis 3 story as an act of rebellion against God. Here is the problem with that, we have sin existing in God's perfection long before the "Fall" took place. We see Adam and Eve as superhuman, and for the most part, they were. They were extremely intelligent beings. God made them in His likeness and image. They tended the whole garden, named the plants and animals. They were SUPER-INTELLIGENT because He created them for communion with Him. In fact, Paul says that God made us above the angels. We will actually judge the angels, and because Satan is a fallen angel, Eve's intellect was far above his. But "knowing" is a far different path than logically reasoning from the ego. Remember the types of fear? One is based on wise understanding and truth, and one is based on a lie. Well, that's what we have here with different types of intelligence. Before Satan confused her, Eve was brilliant. The change happened once she believed the lie and then began processing from intellect based on that lie: I AM NOT WHO GOD SAYS I AM. I

CANNOT TRUST GOD. I NEED TO BE SOME-THING DIFFERENT THAN I AM. Eve was completely innocent, she had absolutely no concept of sin or evil, therefore she could not have been acting out of rebellion. She did not have the "stranger danger" concept drilled into her innocent mind. She was tricked... we have all been tricked, and once we see that, once we really grab hold of the enemy's ploy, we will never be suckered again. The only thing we have to do is agree to forever fast from the fruit of the Tree of the Knowledge of Good and Evil. If you don't know how to do that, just ask God to show you.

Christ already destroyed the separation concept. He already showed us our true identity in Him. He already did all the hard work. We as Christians have based entire theologies on the separation LIE...we are still devouring the forbidden fruit because it makes us feel so smart. But that knowledge is a lie from hell and it can never bear the fruit of the spirit. Make the decision right now to not only allow Christ to restore your innocence, but to permanently seek God's counsel on how to fast from that wretched fruit. He will show you, and once you've found that freedom, you will be amazed at how rotten that fruit tastes if you go back to it (which in the early stages we inevitably do).

Rebellion is the identity the enemy gave Eve, and it is the identity that all of humanity inherited from him. It is a false identity, so don't let anyone tell you that you are a product of your environment. You are a product of the Holiness of God, Christ didn't just teach that, He lived it out and showed us that. Another thing we have been taught is that Christ left his throne in Heaven, came to Earth to save our wretched, sinful souls, and we should not allow ourselves to feel worthy of his sacrifice. Technically, that is true, but the approach is skewed. There is something terribly wrong with that perspective and it hurts us to not get it straight. He did what He did for one reason: Because we are worth it.

If a predator tricked your little child, robbed them of their innocence skewing their minds and bodies, would you shame that child? Of course, not (although victim shaming is a huge problem in our world.). If you had an opportunity to rescue your child, would you call out all the wrong deeds they had committed in the process of maneuvering their dysfunctional logic? Would you shame a victim into appreciating your sacrifice for rescuing them? Do you see how pathetic that is? Eve was innocent, her mind was skewed, her reverent heart was raped and replaced with the most intellectual knowledge of good and evil which serves one purpose only: separation from God. Now, imagine again if your child was abducted and robbed of their innocence. Would you want to reiterate to your child that it wasn't their fault? Would you help them understand how they were tricked? Would you continue all the days of your life securing your child in your love for them, reassuring them that all they have to do is feel the weight of your love for healing? Or would you continue to heap condemnation on them, recounting every evil act they were engaged in? Which one do you think would draw them into your love?

What would you be willing to do to help them trust you? You would love them unconditionally, and that is exactly what Jesus did. It is time to flip the script. It is true that we are 100% responsible for our own behavior, but we need to view our behavior from the position of the finished work of the Cross and not the Tree of the Knowledge of Good and Evil. The enemy is a liar, ain't no good thing ever come out of his mouth.   Do not allow him any headspace. Kick him out once and for all. God will embrace you and love you. And from the position of that secure, Omnipotent love, you will begin to change. You will gain revelation into the darkest parts of your soul, and His light will heal and sustain you. When you are walking in your Christ inherited Holy identity, behavior modification will be unnecessary. Self-righteousness will feel so fake and foreign. The Holy Spirit will soften your heart and create in you a new man, and you will never look back. When you are reminded of your Holy identity, your perspective of the meaning of love will change, and there is not one thing this world will offer you outside of His Love that will be appealing to you. It is crazy how great life can be when you know In Whom You Belong.

One thing to remember is that the enemy doesn't go down without a fight, and that's ok. It is a world reality. We are tempted to get caught up in the battle of good and evil. Again, no knowledge from that fruit can bear spiritual maturity. The knowledge of good is just as evil as the knowledge of evil. This is where self-righteousness comes in. If we are measuring our worth, our value, or establishing an identity in anything other than the Love of God, we are missing the mark and not walking in freedom.

So yes, technically Jesus left His throne and came to earth to save our wretched souls because He loves us and wants us in a right relationship with the Father.   But the script doesn't end there.... He didn't leave Heaven behind,

He brought it with Him and walked it out on Earth. He established the Kingdom right here so you and I can walk in His peace, now! He broke all the barriers so we can share in His abundance now, not just after we die. We can walk in the kingdom now. That is our inherent right. That is our authority... don't buy the lie another day. Step up to the plate, surrender the game and watch what God does for you. So, to make things clearer I want to reiterate some truths.

You are a holy, divine being. God created you that way. Satan tricked you, he abducted you from the Father, and he assaulted you.

No matter who he went through and used to harm you, the source of the abduction is Satan, not the person. They have been tricked too and are operating from the same false identity of rebellion assigned by Satan.

Self-righteousness is a serious sin because it sets us up to deny our need for help and keeps us tethered to a false identity. It too, is an act of rebellion. We will use beliefs, religion, behavior modification, arrogance, comparisons, etc. to prove our worthiness. That is the face of self-righteousness.

There is no freedom in this. I need to stress this because I was lost in this specific sin for a long time. I see so many Christian brethren not walking in their beloved identity and it hurts. We, of all people, should be walking in the Kingdom Jesus established for us. We should be free.

How can we preach the Gospel of Christ to the lost

world if we have not recklessly abandoned ourselves into the resting place of Grace?

Being saved from eternal damnation and entering the Kingdom of Heaven are not exclusively the same thing. You don't have to wait. You can embrace freedom and walk out the Kingdom right here, right now. Jesus did that for us.

Are we worshipping God or are we worshipping doctrine? Are we saved by grace, or are we banking on our own understanding? Are we smarter or better than others because we think we have some special knowledge of good and evil that they don't have?

Hmmm, sound familiar?

Do we know God personally or do we just know a lot about Him?

Have we allowed God intimate knowledge of us?

Have we asked Him to search us and know us, and then show us?

Do we have amazing theories, fantastic theology and well-developed arguments?

Or have we entered so deeply into Grace that we are humbled to oblivion, where there is no I or them... only us and we?

What's the big lie? Satan says, "Eat of this tree and you will be like your dad."

But the truth is, she already was... The spittin' image of her dad.

QUESTIONS FOR CONTEMPLATION

1. Studying Genesis Chapter 3, what was Satan's goal?
2. What was Satan's approach in tricking Eve?
3. Assuming Eve was tricked, how does that contradict the Original Sin Theory?
4. What is Satan's greatest tool?
5. According to Genesis Chapter 3, what was man's first emotion?

————————————————

1. *Merriam-Webster.com Dictionary*, s.v. "fear," accessed February 11, 2022, https://www.merriam-webster.com/dictionary/fear.
   Style: Chicago

THE THIRD GIVE OF FORGIVENESS

GIVE MYSELF (AND ALL MY HURT) OVER TO GOD

T he Bible continually brings reference to dying to the flesh. We all want to die to the flesh, we know the value of being obedient to this truth, but you cannot die to the flesh until you eulogize the emotions. That's half of who you are. We are dual beings. A part of the personality must die, and that is a painful process.

Anytime we are operating from our emotions, we are standing with the EGO (Edging God Out). We cannot operate from and in holy alignment and be steered by our emotions at the same time. So, dying to the self and eulogizing the pain is vital. We must allow ourselves to feel the emotions, and let them teach us what they are supposed to teach us. This is how we honor them. Shoving them down and pretending they do not exist will not work.

We have to feel our emotions, acknowledge them BUT not be led by them. Remove your emotions through awareness. Examine your hurt, examine the one who hurt you, and examine with Godly discernment how you feel about the situations. Contemplate and feel your hurt, then surrender all of that to the only sure justification: GOD. Grieve the process, do not rush it, but also, do not get stuck there. Trust the Holy Spirit to govern the process and create sacred purpose in every ounce of pain.

Giving ourselves over to God is usually a messy process of surrender. It is not in our primitive mind or physical DNA to surrender unless forced. So, we often force His hand. I have said many times, I do not really know how to surrender, but in seeking Him I have definitely learned to be broken. After a few times of doing this, we hope to develop the ability to trust Him without having to suffer needlessly, thus making surrender a more natural part of our daily lives. One thing is for sure, we won't surrender to a God we don't trust, and we won't trust a God we don't know.

So, spending time with Him is crucial for developing a relationship, and burying ourselves in His word reminds us of His promises.

This is a favorite prayer verse about allowing God to know us and trusting His direction.

> [23] *Search me, God, and know my heart;*
>   *test me and know my anxious thoughts.*
> [24] *See if there is any offensive way in me,*
>   *and lead me in the way everlasting.*

> — PSALMS 139:23-24

This is literally saying, "I surrender myself to you for you to show me my error." This is the obvious position of a humbled heart. The only way we can see our error is if we are allowing God to reveal Himself to us and be revealed in us. Only humility can receive that correction. Only from the perspective of His Holiness can we even see our brokenness for what it is. We cannot clearly see sin if we are looking from the position of the law.

The law is a "head game" not a "heart desire." Sin may be pointed out in the law, but it cannot be corrected there. The only right perspective of sin is from the position of Holiness, consumed in Grace... which rests 100% in Agape.

> *The Lord will fight for you; you need only to be still.*
>
> — EXODUS 14:14

One of my favorite sports to watch is UFC. A few years ago, I was watching a preliminary fight and this is where I received a revelation for the acronym "TAP OUT." One of the fighters wore apparel that seemed to suggest his Christian faith. Of course, that sparked my attention as it was familiar to me. In the middle of the fight, he got locked in a choke hold. It was obvious he was struggling, to no avail. He was locked down. He wrestled, twisted, and maneuvered, but the hold was solid. He appeared to be at the point of passing out.

Suddenly, he softened his struggle and went limp. It appeared as though he had been choked out. That was not the case. As soon as he relaxed and quit resisting, his opponent softened the hold. He immediately shifted his position, took advantage of the opponent and managed to flip the fight. He got his opponent in a choke hold and ended up winning the fight as his opponent tapped out.

I received revelation from the Holy Spirit, and an inner dialogue took place. I heard, "Todd, that is what you are doing to me." I paused and responded with, "God, I don't fight you." The reply I received was, "You are resisting me right now, I am trying to teach you." Honestly, I was still stuck on the UFC event and it wasn't sinking in. I could not clearly see how I was fighting God, but I knew the message was powerful so I persisted in being obedient to hearing him. "Todd, I want you to tap out." "I will fight for you, if only you be still."

Submitting to God and surrendering to his authority does not mean the same thing as submitting in the flesh. Guys, this is huge. When we are in the middle of the battle, the last thing that comes to mind is submission. Submitting to God can often feel like surrendering to the enemy. We have to know, that we know who our God is and where our allegiance rests.

The enemy wants a fight. He is poised and ready for battle 24/7, and he has an entire cohort at his disposal. God wants us to TAP OUT. He wants us to trust him completely with our battles. He wants us to trust him and his love for us. He wants us to trust him with our opponents, our enemies, our hurts and our shortcomings. Apart from him we will never know true victory. We will settle for accolades from this world and totally miss the inheritance of the one true King.

"TAP OUT" Part I:

T-*Trust* God with my sin and my life.
A-*Accept* His forgiveness and do not continue to
shame or condemn myself. I AM FORGIVEN?
P-*Peace* will come to me as I begin to see myself

as He sees me: sanctified, holy, and righteous.
It all boils down to one thing: Identity.

> *This righteousness is given through*
> *faith in[a] Jesus Christ to all who*
> *believe. There is no difference between*
> *Jew and Gentile*
>
> — ROMANS 3:22

> *Both the one who makes people holy and those*
> *who are made holy are of the same*
> *family. So, Jesus is not ashamed to call*
> *them brothers and sisters.*
>
> — HEBREWS 2:11

Sin vs. Dispute

One of the coolest things to happen while learning to
surrender ourselves and our hurts over to God is that He
helps us discern the difference between betrayal and misunderstanding. Betrayals need to be forgiven; misunderstand-

ings need to be forgotten. When we are hurting, sometimes misunderstandings feel bigger than they are. We all communicate differently and perceive information through our own filters. Sometimes we have truly just miscommunicated information, and we perceive that misinformation as sin.

One of the most beautiful parts of surrendering to God is how the Holy Spirit reveals the difference to us. How many times have you been misunderstood? Guess what? We are all on both sides of this. Remember, the enemy has one task in life: Destroy relationships. He has a way of using hurt to create dissension and chaos. So, when seeking God's counsel, be open to recognizing the ways misunderstandings and misperceptions are labeled as sin and be ok with being wrong. Sometimes the thing we need to forgive most is our own lack of understanding and foolishly allowing the enemy to use us as a tool to create more conflict! Ouch, ouch...triple ouch!!

> [16] *"No one lights a lamp and hides it in a clay jar or puts it under a bed. Instead, they put it on a stand, so that those who come in can see the light.* [17] *For there is nothing hidden that will not be disclosed, and nothing concealed that will not be known or brought out into the open.* [18] *Therefore consider carefully how you listen. Whoever has will be given more; whoever does not have, even what they think they have will be taken from them."*

— LUKE 8 -A LAMP ON A STAND

TESTIMONY

One of the biggest mistakes we make is feeling bad about feeling bad. There is a huge amount of shame that comes into play when we do not address our humanness and the sheer vulnerability in life. None of us are absolved from being hurt or from hurting others. It is an absolute fact of life. So, accepting it and knowing that it is just ok to hurt is vital. It is not ok to get stuck there and allow that hurt to govern our behavior, thus our lives. And...it is not ok to accept that we must stay in hurtful situations where we are in danger. It is also not ok to pay that hurt forward and use our pain to continue to hurt others.

Discernment is so valuable, and the only way to develop discernment is having a God-centered life, getting to know the Holy Spirit, and allowing Him to reveal our sacred identity. This understanding rustled within me a need to get deep down into the source of my own suffering. Through petitioning and prayer, I began to feel an unusual connection with the Holy Spirit.

Look at how John addressed this topic:

> *25 "These things I have spoken to you while*
> *being present with you. 26 But the Helper,*
> *the Holy Spirit, whom the Father*
> *will send in My name, He will teach you*
> *all things, and bring to your remem-*
> *brance all things that I said to*

> *you. ²⁷ Peace I leave with you, My peace I*
> *give to you; not as the world gives do I*
> *give to you. Let not your heart be trou-*
> *bled, neither let it be afraid.*
>
> — JOHN 14:25-27 NKJV

I relied heavily upon this promise and trusted Jesus with the work of healing that was taking place. I relied solely upon the help of the Holy Spirit to guide me. While sleeping, I started getting glimpses of my childhood, and memories of events and people started flowing. It was a period of time when some of the most painful situations of my life began to unfold. I'm not going to lie here, this was hard. It was painful. It was scary and it hurt. Of all the things I suffered as a child, nothing was more scarring than being abused by my own mother. The one person I had once been able to trust and should have been able to count on for comfort, at some point turned on me. I was just a little boy.

Jesus says if you hate your brother, you have killed them in your heart. Boy, I must have killed my mom a thousand times. The Holy Spirit was beginning to do a work in me by revealing some really dark events in dream state glimpses. Every time I would wake up from a dream, I would be so pissed off.

I remembered once when my mom made me strip naked, spanked me, and had me stand naked in front of her lady friends. I was about 7 years old. She made me stand butt naked and apologize to them for my behavior which was really just normal childlike behavior. The spanking and then smeared humiliation of being bare before her and her friends? What in all of hell was that about? It was a deeper shame that rose up. Spanking may be a legitimate way to get a child's attention if they are doing something wrong, but this was different. This was gross humiliation and totally uncalled for. The process of learning to forgive was truly the result of being obedient to the Word of God and allowing the Holy Spirit to work forgiveness in me and through me. I began to see deeper into the situations of my childhood but from the perspective of an adult. I was able to address this from both perspectives actually, which helped that child gain understanding and begin the process of healing.

During my mom's divorce from dad, something caused her to flip. Something in her really changed, she was not always abusive. These are things God started showing me. It started in dreams, I would catch glimpses of our life, and each memory offered insight into a scenario. It was like connecting dots through reels of memory. My misbehavior started making sense to me, as the scales fell away from my eyes, healing began. I began to see the reasons for my poor behavior and then mom's poor behavior began to make sense, then dad's. Then I remembered being sexually assaulted at a younger age by a man at the Boys Club. As I am gradually but surely processing all this, the Holy Spirit helps me gain insight into the predatory behavior of that perpetrator. I began to see the whole world differently.

Once the veil was torn away, I saw my holy identity and I no longer viewed all the events through the veil of lies. Witnessing through my own vulnerability, I was able to first see my sacred value and then the value of all involved. The revelation was immediate, but processing that revelation took a while. More things kept coming. In dream after dream, the Holy Spirit brought new understanding which helped with surrender and healing. The Holy Spirit finally gave me the revelation I needed: it wasn't my fault. None of it was my fault. Whoever you are, wherever you are and whatever happened to you, you probably need to know that too. The exploitation of your innocence was not your fault! Whether it was sexual abuse, mental and emotional abuse, or any other manipulative behavior that caused you to doubt yourself or not feel lovable, it was not your fault. Let that sink in, and allow yourself to grieve. Ask God for a deeper revelation into your innocence as guided by your relationship with the Holy Spirit. You will be amazed at just how willing He is to draw you nearer.

All along I continued to receive glimpses of conversations mom had with family and friends. I began to see how generational suffering traveled through our family. I reeled in her frustrating words of being passed over for promotion after promotion at her work. She took great pride in her work and was educated far beyond what was required. Her expertise was greater than the men she worked for as well as the men she trained who continued gaining promotions ahead of her. I saw the pain and anguish in her face as she tried to figure out ways to get ahead as a pregnant, single mother of two, living in a world where divorce was still an ugly shame and women were expected to marry for security, not advance in the workforce. I began remembering conversations she had with her boss, asking for more responsibility so she could advance. I clearly recalled hearing her pleading with him, highlighting her qualifications, explaining her need as a single mother, and questioning why she was being passed over by men less qualified than her. Can you imagine being told, "These men have families to feed, and you can just get married if you want to get ahead?" My mom was brilliant, and she was constantly squashed in a society that had no capacity for her. It became clear to me that I was the only "male" in her life who she could control, and I caught it all. She took it all out on me. Although nothing can erase the shame and guilt I felt as a child at the hands of her abuse, there came a peace within me as I realized we all hurt one another for the same reason: because we have been hurt, and we do not know how to hurt successfully or what to do with the pain. Instead of learning how to hurt, learning how to move forward in forgiveness, we often lash out forcing our pain back onto those who hurt us, or more often we pay it forward to people totally innocent to us. I wanted to forgive. I wanted to be free. I realized I was, like so many others, collateral damage. But I didn't want to get stuck there. So, through God's graceful leading into the memory of my youth, and with the comfort offered from the comforter himself, the Holy Spirit, I was led to explore one event after another.

This began in me the process of self-examination, self-love, and self-forgiveness. I have hurt a lot of people... A LOT. I have been hurt many times over, and I dare say that forgiving myself has been the most difficult process. Learning to forgive "ME" for the ways I paid hurt back and the ways I paid it forward has been most challenging. I went from seeing myself as the victim and seeing my mom as the offender, to saying out loud, "Oh my God, we are really just alike." The inability to see our true, innate Christ nature, clouds our boundaries. We often accept responsibility for the actions of others, which leads to the development of a controlling nature. And/Or we maintain a victim mentality and begin blaming others for our actions. Forgiving the self is challenging in this sense because it requires the recognition of boundaries, responsibility, and accountability. This is the basis for systemic generational bondage: the inability to see, thus forgive our own wrongs. Ultimately, self-forgiveness brings us to necessary surrender. From this place, we can get deep into the ministry of Jesus. Self-forgiveness is at the root of the freedom He offers and requires radical obedience and surrender to His love.

It is my duty and privilege in prayer, to call forth the Love of God into this broken, hurting world, and an honor to share these revelations as guided by the Holy Spirit.

-Todd

Believe God's truth about my identity

> *Thanks be to God, who delivers me through*
> *Jesus Christ our Lord! So then, I myself*
> *in my mind am a slave to God's law, but*
> *in my sinful nature a slave to the law*
> *of sin.*

— Romans 7:25

What we have to remember is that we will never be able

to keep the law, and in trying to do so we risk being pulled away from grace. The only good that can come from our effort is hopefully we get to the end of ourselves and finally surrender. That's what I mean by being broken. We can't do anything, and I mean NOT ONE THING apart from grace. And receiving grace requires surrender. The best part about grace is entering into the rest of agape. THIS IS OUR TRUE IDENTITY. This is the place where sin has no hold because this is the place where the false identity assigned to us by Satan is exposed for what it is...A BIG FAT LIE.

The world gives us all kinds of roles and identities, none of which are sacred or holy. If we are honest with ourselves, worldly roles and identities are all aimed at one thing: controlling people or outcomes. The carnal world does not even understand the Kingdom of Heaven thus cannot perpetuate anything sacred or holy. This primitive world needs roles so it can keep up the game of sin through false identities. Once we adopt and accept agape as our true inheritance, nothing this world offers us will be appealing. We will be able to enjoy all the ways Kingdom living helps us see and experience the abundant life. We can still live in the world, enjoying the sensory experiences of the flesh but doing so from the place of holy completeness. It is amazing how much more we can enjoy drinking wine, eating fresh foods, sexual pleasure, etc. when experiencing God's ordained purpose. Having been on both sides of this, I can tell you there is nothing more pleasurable than receiving His sacred intention. The enemy can only counterfeit what God intended. The enemy will always exploit, control and demand ownership through deceitful mimics. With Jesus, we are allowed to share in everything with Him, and he doesn't take and take and take. He gives sacrificially to anyone who would choose to experience all the pleasures of this world with Him. What a mighty revelation is this?

Forgiveness is the hinge of reconciliation with our Creator. This reconciled identity is the place where raging wars inside a man come to a dead stop; where the lust for revenge and all the demons which summon enmity, decidedly fade away. For the Christian who wants to live in total freedom from this world, radical forgiveness is not a casual suggestion. Radical forgiveness will require a kind of self-death that few people are willing to experience. BUT it is the only inroad for the abundant life promised by Jesus Christ.

REMOVE MY DOUBT

> *28 "Lord, if it's you," Peter replied, "tell me to come to you on the water." 29 "Come," he said. Then Peter got down out of the boat, walked on the water, and came toward Jesus. 30 But when he saw the wind, he was afraid and, beginning to sink, cried out, "Lord, save me!" 31 Immediately Jesus reached out his hand and caught him. "You of little faith," he said, "why did you doubt?"*
>
> — MATTHEW 14:28-31

When we get down to the nitty-gritty, digging up the root source of our pain, we will find that it is less about the grievance, the insult, and the offense and more about our lack of faith. It's ok, this should not shame us. Ask anyone who has a deep, unmoving faith, and you will hear the testimony of persevering through waves of pain and doubt. Pain forces us to make changes. Pain forces us to alter our perspective of everything, mostly ourselves and God. If we maneuver doubt and fear with grace and solely seek the Kingdom of Heaven, we are guaranteed a successful outcome.

However, if our answer is ill will toward those who hurt us, we will continue to battle the situation the enemy stirred up. Take note of the Hebrews account of entering or not entering into the place of rest.

> *Therefore, since the promise of entering his rest still stands, let us be careful that none of you be found to have fallen short of it. [2] For we also have had the good news proclaimed to us, just as they did; but the message they heard was of no value to them, because they did not share the faith of those who obeyed. [3] Now we who have believed enter that rest, just as God has said,*
> *"So, I declared on oath in my anger, They shall never enter my rest."*
> *And yet his works have been finished since the creation of the world. [4] For somewhere he has spoken about the seventh day in these*

words: "On the seventh day God rested from all his works." [5] And again in the passage above he says, "They shall never enter my rest."

[6] Therefore since it still remains for some to enter that rest, and since those who formerly had the good news proclaimed to them did not go in because of their disobedience, [7] God again set a certain day, calling it "Today." This he did when a long time later he spoke through David, as in the passage already quoted:
"Today, if you hear his voice,
  do not harden your hearts."

[8] For if Joshua had given them rest, God would not have spoken later about another day. [9] There remains, then, a Sabbath-rest for the people of God; [10] for anyone who enters God's rest also rests from their works,[1] just as God did from his. [11] Let us, therefore, make every effort to enter that rest, so that no one will perish by following their example of disobedience.

[12] For the word of God is alive and active. Sharper than any double-edged sword, it penetrates even to dividing soul and spirit, joints and marrow; it judges the thoughts and attitudes of the heart. [13] Nothing in all creation is hidden from God's sight. Everything is

*uncovered and laid bare before the eyes of
him to whom we must give account.*

— HEBREWS 4:1-13

Examining this particular scripture, it is blatantly apparent that to not choose rest is to choose disobedience. We need to pause here and examine what we consider sin to be. If sin is defined as "missing the mark," then doubt, fear, unforgiveness, and withholding love are all based on a sinful or limiting mindset. While we are obviously learning to call out to God to help us be obedient in our seeking His Kingdom and highest good, we must remember to keep the focus on cultivating purity in our own hearts and minds.

Forgiveness is not an option if obedience is desired. Actually, to not forgive is to continue to live with doubt and fear. We may mask this fear as a false identity and mock strength, but it is actually in direct rebellion to the freedom God has for us. So, while we think our unforgiveness is directed at those who hurt us, the enemy knows something we don't always see. He knows if he can stir up our emotions, help us feel indignant and self-righteous, he can not only be in control of our situations, our mindset, and our immediate relationships, he can actually alter how we see and relate to God. I have to be honest with you here. THIS is the source of all our pain; this lack of faith and rebellion against the love of God. Choosing forgiveness is a radical act of obedience. It is not saying that the offense or insult is okay, it is saying that only God can take the mess of betrayal and make it holy.

If we expect to receive the gift of his promises and experience agape, we must surrender, fully knowing that those "other people," who hurt us so badly are welcome to receive Him as well. It is not saying, "What happened to me is ok." It is saying, "I do not have the full picture as does God, and my desire is that His love is known at all costs." That cost being, laying down our pride and trusting God fully with the outcome. God does not withhold His rest from anyone. Though not resting in Him will feel like wrath, we must understand this is our choice. We must make the choice to align ourselves with Him if we expect freedom. The same freedom offered to us is also offered to those we perceive as our enemies. It is a win/win for the Kingdom and a lose/lose for the real enemy, the principalities of evil. Sin is its own punishment, and that punishment comes from not resting in agape. Whatever offense is against you, just know, the inability to surrender yourself and your pain to God is also a sin that keeps you from His healing love. Ask yourself this question:

Why would I not choose forgiveness? There are many reasons a person may choose to hang on to grievances. For me, there were two themes that continued to rear up as resistance to the Love of God. First, is the idea that by not forgiving, I could somehow make sure that this "thing" would never happen to me again. That's a flat-out lie. Unforgiveness is a sure way to cycle right back around to the same or a similar situation. It may be a different time with different people and different circumstances, but you will likely repeat a cyclical pattern. Secondly, having a victim mentality. The problem with holding onto a victim mentality is that we never examine our own behavior. Now, don't get me wrong, we can never accept responsibility for the actions of others. Victim shaming is never ok. But, we can get so caught up in being a victim that we fail to see the part we often play in our own messes. We fail to accept responsibility for our own actions. If we are caught up in cyclical patterns of dysfunction, it is our responsibility to claim a victory over our own thinking. Let's say it this way: Your life is 100% your responsibility. The only way to be successful (from a Godly perspective of success bearing the fruit of the Spirit) is to press into Him, not rely on our own understanding, thus allowing Him more and more access and eventually trusting the Holy Spirit to govern us.

TESTIMONY

Experiencing a very public and somewhat painful divorce from my husband of 29 years, I found it difficult to remember the beauty of surrender. While I can say with confidence that I do seek God with all my heart, I can also recognize the painful ways maturing into the fullness of grace is a messy business. And though the intent of my heart is pure, the way that pain rushes forth uninhibited has left me at times, not so humble. Actually, I can be more honest than that. I became indignant and prideful. This happens when we take offense. Fear does that to us. When we are hurting, especially in the presence of betrayal, we develop a self-awareness that may easily become self-right-eousness. We basically get stuck in the hurt and develop a false identity around a mock strength which makes it impossible to see our own failures. I am now and will always be a work in progress that makes the seeking phases of finding the "peace that passes understanding," the most beautiful part of the journey.

While divorce at any level is painful and messy and gut-wrenching it doesn't have to end there.... or even pause there. Those times are actually part of the seeking and ultimately pivotal in finding and creating the all-new creature God wants each of us to be. When studying yoga, I learned unique teachings and practical meditations for finding joy in suffering and actually allowing that suffering to cultivate within us a deeper joy. Christ actually taught this, he lived it and gave the ultimate gift to us in his death and resurrection so that we would have tangible evidence of our true identity.

Under His authority, our innate sovereignty emerges and we are suddenly able to see His Kingdom at hand. We develop a supernatural ability to not conform to the patterns of this world but actually choose the higher road. He left us a comforter in the Holy Spirit who is just waiting to show us an all-new way of maneuvering the pathways of life that feel like a slow-burning hell. All we have to do is ask. The Holy Spirit is not some abstract being, he is tangible and recognizable, and if you find yourself ravaged with pain, he will fall upon you a level of comfort and peace that the world cannot even begin to understand much less mimic.

I can't say it takes the pain away, it is more of a sooth-ing. But in that soothing, as we learn to surrender, the pain subsides and is replaced with a strength that could not be cultivated any other way. As I was coming to the end of assisting my brother Todd with this book, I found it not coincidental that I would be suffering so deeply and realizing that all my relief, all my joy, and all my hope rests on one thing only: the ability to surrender, allowing God to wash me clean of all pride bringing me into and out of the grave of self-righteousness and have me emerge, resurrecting all new. We have the promise of life abundantly if we don't lose focus. If we don't project our pain and if we don't lose faith in the power of LOVE, we will feel and know the absolute freedom that comes with: "forgive us Father, we don't know what we are doing."

-Kacy

QUESTIONS FOR CONTEMPLATION

1. Based on all we have studied thus far WHY do we struggle with sin?
2. What does Jesus say about us?
3. What does Satan say about us?
4. Who are we listening to and why?
5. Do you now understand why we are all in the same boat?
6. CAN you trust God enough to accept His forgiveness and forgive yourself?

The Fourth Give of Forgiveness

Give my enemies over to God.

Giving our enemies over to God. What does that look like in our everyday life? And why is it so hard to do? We all have an innate desire for justice. It is written on our hearts, encoded in our DNA. When someone betrays us or harms us, the first thought is usually geared toward seeing them pay somehow.

Honestly, the deepest human desire is to have some redemption in the face of darkness. We bring closure to a hurtful situation through repentance, and then we sink into redemption. But things don't always go that way. What if we receive no apology? Most people who seek to betray or harm others have already justified their behavior and may go on living like it never happened. So, what do we do with that? What if our enemies are thriving and are boastful or even glad to have hurt us? What if there is no regret, remorse, or repentance? What if they continue to try and hurt us even more? What then? How can there be redemption where there is no repentance?

This is important because if we aren't careful, we can

get caught up in a game of cat and mouse and allow ourselves to be lured into a deeper pattern of deceit, totally losing our alignment with God.

So, what do we do? We take our grievance to God and surrender it, allowing the full weight of responsibility to rest in His promises to defend us. We make a conscious choice to ask Him to show us how to forgive. We allow Him to guide us toward closure, and in the process teach us self-forgiveness. We do this for one reason and one reason only: to be pleasing to Him, knowing His truth brings us freedom. We don't do it so that we can control any part of the situation. We do it as an act of obedience so we stay in alignment with Him, trusting fully that He will take it and work it for our good. We accept that the only reconciliation we should be concerned with is reconciling our hurt with His Love. Some relationships can heal, mature, and grow with trials and betrayals. Some absolutely cannot.

There are those who do not need access to us or our lives. In the midst of pain, trial and chaos, we may not always be able to discern who should and should not be in our lives. So, surrendering our enemies over to God is vital. He and He alone knows who can be a productive part of our growth and who will hinder us or continue to seek harm against us. This is challenging and must be met with conviction and resolve. This doesn't mean we shouldn't pray for our enemies. It means we should let God have the final say and not resist His authority.

There is overwhelming freedom that falls on us when we are able to do this. When we allow God to rearrange our hearts and minds, He begins rearranging our lives, and the way His love begins to manifest all around us will be astounding. It can actually be a little unnerving at first, as unnecessary conflict gets erased and new patterns of life emerge. As our spiritual countenance changes, so with it the mind, will, and emotions are altered to be more like Jesus. I need to be perfectly honest here. As beautiful as this whole process is, it can also be a little weird. Actually, it can be really weird. Sometimes when asking for change, we don't realize how reliant we have become upon dysfunctional patterns. When those patterns are disrupted and new patterns begin to develop, it will often and most likely feel as though we are walking on foreign ground. That is a valid feeling because we are playing on all-new turf. So, remember it takes time, dedication, and focus. We must stay buried in His Word and rely heavily on His promises.

Earlier in the book, there was a statement made: Facts of the flesh will rarely, if ever, align with God's promises. We must learn to discern that which is true in the carnal world around us, is not the same as His Absolute Truth. We will be pivoting back and forth until the scales over our eyes are fully peeled away. Sometimes, we won't even know what we believe about anything. Remember, that's a good place to be. It positions us to dig deeper, ask more questions and begin to see the fruition of the Truth born of His promises. During these transitions, we often feel like we are failing at everything. Discouragement will come and be overwhelming at times, but we have a plan. The plan is to allow the Love of God to be our foundational Truth and disallow anything that speaks against it.

> [27] *"But to you who are listening I say: Love*
> *your enemies, do good to those who hate*

you, ²⁸ bless those who curse you, pray for
those who mistreat you.

— LUKE 6:27-28

¹⁷ Do not repay anyone evil for evil. Be
careful to do what is right in the eyes of
everyone. ¹⁸ If it is possible, as far as it
depends on you, live at peace with every-
one. ¹⁹ Do not take revenge, my dear
friends, but leave room for God's wrath,
for it is written: "It is mine to avenge; I
will repay,"[a] says the Lord.

— ROMANS 12:17-19

Praying for our enemies is a principle that requires meditation and discernment. The same love that sets us free, sets our perceived enemy free. One reason we have such a hard time with forgiveness is we want "those people" to pay for what they did to us. Think about this for a minute. If it is true that we reap what we sow, then sowing revenge and recompense just invite it back on us. This is why God says to love those who hate us. He knows we cannot do that without Him, which brings us to surrender and ultimately into His rest. He knows the only way to remove the enemy and bring providential grace into the entirety of the situation is for Him to have full authority.

Unforgiveness keeps us tied to the grievance, and guess what? It does not hurt the other person at all. God's grace and love are equally available to everyone. It only hurts us to not forgive because unforgiveness forms a barrier preventing us from receiving grace in the grievance. In the Christian life, we are called to serve and be selfless. This is the only and greatest act of love where we are not only allowed but commanded to be totally selfish: Forgiveness. We do this for ourselves and our own freedom.

Have you ever wondered why we have such a hard time surrendering our enemies? ***Because we want to be in control***, but we aren't. We are not in control of all the circumstances in our own lives much less the lives of others. Control is a spirit and a lying spirit. Don't fall for it. The only thing we can control is our willingness to surrender to the One who is in control. WE CAN HONOR OUR HURT BY BURYING OURSELVES WITH IT IN TOTAL SURRENDER AND ALLOWING OURSELVES TO EMERGE ALL NEW. We can only do this by trusting the omnipotent love of God. Keep in mind, that unforgiveness holds the insult close, the wounds raw and keeps the scabs tender. Unforgiveness clouds our view and thus predicates the decisions we make for everything in our lives.

Can you see how cyclical patterns are created? Unforgiveness is at the root of everything. If the result of our actions is not total freedom from the desired outcome, then the motivation is not honest. Let's get real here. How many of our decisions are clouded with a desire to control the results and outcomes? The answer is likely MOST ALL, especially where hurt is involved! Dig deep here. The root of this is fear, the spirit involved is control, and with a little more digging you will find it often comes down to unforgiveness.

WHO OF US IS WITHOUT SIN?

Jesus walked up the Mount of Olives near the city where he spent the night. *² Then at dawn Jesus appeared in the temple courts again, and soon all the people gathered around to listen to his words, so he sat down and taught them. ³ Then in the middle of his teaching, the religious scholars and the Pharisees broke through the crowd and brought a woman who had been caught in the act of committing adultery and made her stand* in the middle *of everyone.*

⁴ Then they said to Jesus, "Teacher, we caught this woman in the very act of adultery. ⁵ Doesn't Moses' law command us to stone to death a woman like this? Tell us, what do you say we should do with her?" ⁶ They were only testing Jesus because they hoped to trap him with his own words and accuse him of breaking the laws of Moses.

But Jesus didn't answer them. Instead, he simply bent down and wrote in the dust with his finger. ⁷ Angry, they kept insisting that he answer their question, so Jesus stood up and looked at them and said, "Let's have the man who has never had a sinful desire] throw the first stone

at her." [8] *And then he bent over again*
and wrote some more words in the dust.
[9] *Upon hearing that, her accusers slowly left*
the crowd one at a time, beginning with
the oldest to the youngest, with a
convicted conscience. [10] *Until finally,*
Jesus was left alone with the woman still
standing there in front of him. So he
stood back up and said to her, "Dear
woman, where are your accusers? Is there
no one here to condemn you?"
[11] *Looking around, she replied, "I see no one,*
Lord."
Jesus said, "Then I certainly don't condemn
you either. Go, and from now on, be free
from a life of sin."

— JOHN 8 PASSION TRANSLATION

This passage is a perfect example of Jesus teaching the importance and power of forgiveness. While it is vital to discern spirits and judge behavior, it is equally important to not judge people. Adultery is a deep betrayal and for the believer, it is in complete rebellion to the teachings of Jesus, but as you can see here Jesus is saying adultery is not any viler or more wrong than any other sin. When we are so quick to condemn and hell-bent on staying conscious of the sins of others, we overlook our own wrongs. OUCH! Who else does this? Jesus was able to impress upon those around Him, they need to stay aligned with God and His will by

staying focused on His love for us. That is our true identity... AGAPE.

Jesus lived it out loud. Sin is its own punishment; we
don't have to constantly point it out and heap condemnation upon one another. People living in rebellion to God
and his love have decidedly chosen carnality over freedom.
No matter how the world makes it appear, sin brings death
and misery; it is its own punishment. We don't need to
scream it with a bullhorn. Believe it or not, it is absolutely
possible to love someone even when they seem lost.

We may have to establish firm boundaries or even cut
off all contact, but we can continue to choose love and
forgiveness. When seeking to forgive, it is important to
remember we are doing it for God. We are doing it because
we want to be obedient. We want our actions and our lives
to be pleasing to God and we want HIS FREEDOM
FROM THIS WORLD. We choose forgiveness when it
doesn't make sense. We choose forgiveness when it still
hurts to choose it.

Choosing forgiveness is choosing God. We know that
by choosing to be radically obedient, God will honor our
pain and bring us into deeper intimacy with Him. We do it
because it is the only way to be nurtured into the peace that
passes all understanding. We forgive those who have hurt us
because HE FORGAVE US. Remember, God is using our
circumstances to bring us closer to Him.

We cannot wait for others to change. We cannot allow
our peace and joy to be contingent upon the behavior of
others. God wants the entirety of his child...every last bit.
He doesn't want us to settle. He can be glorified in the

worst of the worst. We just have to surrender and trust, and let the Holy Spirit do His work in us.

> [28] *And we know that in all things God works*
> *for the good of those who love him,*
> *who have been called according to his*
> *purpose.*

> — ROMANS 8:28

Take note here, ALL MEANS ALL. When we are called to His purpose, He works everything for our good. Yes, even the deepest betrayals when surrendered in forgiveness will become the bedrock of our triumph. One thing to note, this will not likely happen overnight. Betrayal hurts, that pain is real. Sometimes we have to surrender several times each day. Remember, forgiveness is a radical act of obedience.

We choose it because we know our relief from the pain rests in our ability to let go. However, the actual healing which leads to a total surrender is something the Holy Spirit does for us. We just have to keep choosing Jesus, keep choosing surrender, and keep choosing agape at all costs.

Eventually, we are rinsed so clean of all the ramifications of insult, we can truly rest in agape. This is a promise guys, not a fairy tale. The Kingdom of Heaven is a tangible place right here, right now. Jesus did that for us, don't believe anything or anyone who says differently. He really did overcome the world, and we have the honor and privilege to be able to walk in that freedom.

WALK IN THE SPIRIT

> [22] But the fruit of the Spirit is love, joy,
> peace, forbearance, kindness, goodness,
> faithfulness, [23] gentleness and self-
> control. Against such things there is
> no law.
>
> — GALATIANS 5:22-23

Have you ever wondered if you are in alignment with God? This is how you know. It is not a big mystery or difficult formula. Galatians 5 points out the fruit produced from the Tree of Life. This is the fruit we should be enjoying. Remember earlier when we talked about the corrupt fruit from the Tree of the Knowledge of Good and Evil. Think about what the fruit of that tree is compared to the fruit of the Spirit. KNOWLEDGE=CONTROL. It is a spirit of fear that keeps us desiring CONTROL. This desire keeps us from trusting and surrendering. It keeps us attached and tethered to cyclical patterns of dysfunction and all the deceitful manifestations born from thinking (knowledge) that we are or even can be in control.

The fruits of the spirit can manifest only one way: GIVING UP, GIVING IN, TOTALLY SURREN-DERING TO AGAPE. This kind of freedom is not just a lofty idea reserved for saints and mystics. It is the tangible fruit of building a relationship with the One in whom you belong. Satan's number one objective is to try and control God. He knows he can't and never will, so he uses the one thing God loves more than anything else: YOU & ME. He destroys our self-perception, then our relational perceptions, and ultimately our perspective of God. How beautiful the finished work of Jesus looks when viewing it from this light. He really suffered, he really died and he really rose again all for one reason only:

A love so great that it could only be revealed through an act of forgiving the most scandalous betrayal of all time.

Yeah, He did that for us. He tore the veil, removed the scales, ripped the blinders away, and restored our vision. Our true, original design of HOLINESS and ONENESS. Satan never stood a chance. Just stop listening to his hissing, negative mind chatter, and self-loathing schemes. You Really Are As Free As You Want To Be...just Look For The Lie. Stop making agreements with the enemy. He is a liar and there is no truth in him. If you are not free, if you are not at peace, if you are not resting, you are listening to the wrong voice. Christ is the redeemer, not the accuser. Be mindful of the inner dialogue of condemnation of self and others.

No matter how much we want others to pay for the insults against us it is important to remember: If Jesus doesn't win then no one wins. We cannot wish ill upon people and expect that to not come back on us. The same love of God that frees us also frees our enemies. One thing we must remember is that we too are the enemy in someone else's story. We all have things we need to be forgiven for. Again, this is an area of personal growth in which the Holy Spirit will bring mature discernment. True forgiveness begins with humility.

> *⁴⁴ But I say to you, love your enemies, bless those who curse you, do good to those who hate you, and pray for those who spitefully use you and persecute you.*
>
> — MATTHEW 5:44 NKJV

Talk about a radical act of obedience!! Just how committed are we to exemplifying the Love of God? Are we able to address a betrayal the way 1 Corinthians 13 suggests?

> *1 If I could speak all the languages of earth and of angels, but didn't love others, I would only be a noisy gong or a clanging cymbal. 2If I had the gift of prophecy, and if I understood all of God's secret plans and possessed all knowledge, and if I had such faith that I could move mountains, but didn't love others, I would be nothing. 3If I gave everything I have to the poor and even sacrificed my body, I could boast about it; but if I didn't love others, I would have gained nothing.*
>
> *4Love is patient and kind. Love is not jealous or boastful or proud 5or rude. It does not demand its own way. It is not irritable, and it keeps no record of being wronged. 6It does not rejoice about injustice but rejoices whenever the truth wins out. 7Love never gives up, never loses*

*faith, is always hopeful, and endures
through every circumstance.*
*8Prophecy and speaking in unknown
languages and special knowledge will
become useless. But love will last forever! 9Now our knowledge is partial and
incomplete, and even the gift of prophecy
reveals only part of the whole
picture! 10But when the time of perfection comes, these partial things will
become useless.*
*11When I was a child, I spoke and thought
and reasoned as a child. But when I grew
up, I put away childish things. 12Now
we see things imperfectly, like puzzling
reflections in a mirror, but then we will
see everything with perfect clarity. All
that I know now is partial and incomplete, but then I will know everything
completely, just as God now knows me
completely.*
*13Three things will last forever—faith, hope,
and love—and the greatest of these is
love.*

Is the Bible ambiguous here or does it mean what it
says? It matters not how polished, holy and right we are.
Unless we have absolved ourselves from this world, surrendered to the love of God, and emulate that, then nothing
we do will be authentic. Unless the motivation behind our
action is love, then we are "missing the mark."

This does not mean allowing abuse, mistreatment, or exploitation. We must learn to discern relationships that dishonor us and establish boundaries with those who harm us. But we do not need to try and control others or their actions. It is futile, it is distracting, and it is WRONG. We simply choose total resignation from the situation and allow God to do His job as our defender. It is not our job to wrestle with someone else's wrong. That is a form of control rooted in dysfunctional logic. Remember, the enemy wants it to be "all about him all the time." If the enemy can convince us to be sin-conscious, he can breed in us a desire to wrestle with him. A full surrender back to the Love of God is what is required. We don't need to know all the ins and outs of the workings of evil. We need only know God's word and His love in ourselves.

All angst comes from wrestling the absolute truth that "we are not in control." If we pray into forgiveness with any sense of entitlement or desired outcomes, for things to go "our way," then we are not praying with honesty or authenticity, and there is no depth or freedom in our forgiveness. Praying through forgiveness (or anything actually) must be a place of total trust, surrendering fully to the sovereignty of God. A place where we meet Jesus, completely sinking with a willingness to be immersed in the single authority of His providential grace. We enter peace, giving in to that sacred home where all angst, fear, vengeance, and pain willfully cries out, "not my will but yours." Anything less is manipulation that will hijack the law of grace. We cannot give something we have not received. And we cannot receive something we have not freely given.

. . .

CS Lewis said it like this:

> But there must be a real giving up of the self.
> You must throw it away
> "blindly" so to speak. Christ will indeed give
> you a real personality: but you must not
> go to Him for the sake of that. As long as
> your own personality is what you are
> bothering about you are not going to
> Him at all. The very first step is to try to
> forget about the self altogether. Your real,
> new self (which is Christ's and also yours,
> and yours just because it is His) will not
> come as long as you are looking for it. It
> will come when you are looking for Him.
> Does that sound strange? The same prin-
> ciple holds, you know, for more everyday
> matters. Even in social life, you will
> never make a good impression on other
> people until you stop thinking about what
> sort of impression you are making. Even
> in literature and art, no man who
> bothers about originality will ever be
> original: whereas if you simply try to tell
> the truth (without caring twopence how
> often it has been told before) you will,
> nine times out of ten, become original
> without ever having noticed it. The prin-
> ciple runs through all life from top to
> bottom. Give up yourself, and you will
> find your real self. Lose your life and you

*will save it. Submit to death, death of
your ambitions and favourite wishes
every day, and death of your whole body
in the end: submit with every fibre of
your being, and you will find eternal
life. Keep back nothing. Nothing that
you have not given away will ever be
really yours. Nothing in you that has not
died will ever be raised from the dead.
Look for yourself, and you will find in
the long run only hatred, loneliness,
despair, and rage ruin and decay. But
look for Christ and you will find Him,
and with Him, everything else thrown in.*

— C.S. LEWIS, MERE CHRISTIANITY

For as a man thinketh so is he.

— PROVERBS 23:7A

Where is our thinking? Where is our focus? God and
God alone can exact judgment. Not one of us has the
knowledge and authority to do this. We can rest knowing
that He is perfect and mighty in all His ways, and we need
to not lose focus on Whom it is we serve. I WANT TO
DRIVE THIS POINT HOME: THIS DOES NOT
MEAN WE ALLOW OURSELVES TO BE BOUND IN
COMPROMISING SITUATIONS. It is the exact opposite. Once we realize we are not and can never be in control,
we will clearly see the "way out" of our conflict. Our desire

to control others is usually the reason we cannot move forward and out of binding circumstances.

Our way out is full surrender of the people who create grief for us and the harmful situations playing out. I know it is cliché but so true: LET GO AND LET GOD. Until we are willing to choose freedom over the need to control, we will settle for betrayal and manipulation. Do you know where this begins? It begins with not knowing our true identity. It begins with us relating too heavily with our carnal man and abandoning our original Self, our Christ nature; our true, holy sacred SELF. Self-betrayal and self-abandonment: these are fruits of unforgiveness.

Can God use us in his justification? Of course, he can. There may be times in more serious circumstances when we are called to stand for truth and justice and make declarations over someone's poor behavior. We have an entire legal system devoted to justice and we need to understand how that system works. More importantly, we need to remember that in order for God to use us, we must be in surrender to him. Otherwise, we can become ravaged with a desire for control or vengeance. The last thing we want is to become a pawn in the enemy's game. Most of us have witnessed this or even experienced it in our own lives. Without being grounded in forgiveness we can't truly surrender, and if we aren't fully surrendered, we are hindering God's justice and blessings.

"TAP OUT" PART II

T-**Trust** God with the ones who have hurt me by allowing

Him to deliver just consequences and exact judgment.
A-*Accept* His decision and His dealings with those who
have hurt me; knowing His plan and my plan for them may
likely be different.
P-*Peace* will come to me when I release myself from these
people and free myself from the chains that have bound me
to the events that have caused so much pain.

THE VEIL IS TORN

Contemplating the final work of Jesus, we see his answer for
everything: humility. He, who had every cause and right,
never once exhibited self-righteousness. Why would we
assume the right to do so? Many will be saved from the
outer darkness, but not all of them will enter the Kingdom
of Heaven. To do so would require laying down the fight,
releasing the carnal man to death, and allowing a resurrection so fresh and new, we would be unrecognizable to the
world. Communion. The world will mock this. The world
will shame this. The carnal world knows only one thing:
self-preservation at all costs where it is all about me all the
time. Sound familiar?

The carnal world has its own playbook, and we become
puppets in the show. We become slaves of the egocentric
master. When we are caught up in our carnal logic, we can't
truly consider how our actions affect others. The person
focused on the flesh will continue through cycles of hurting
others in an effort to have their own needs met. And the
"world" has every carnal pleasure known to man promising
fulfillment. It becomes a cycle of me and mine. Until there
is a full surrender to the Love of God, there is no chance of

lasting peace. This is challenging for everyone. Be reminded, as you draw closer to God, closer to your true identity, and deeper into the life He has for you, some people will not go with you. You will begin to witness a struggle within, as the carnal mind tries to maintain control. This gets messy at times, but God always provides helpers. It is amazing to me how the Body of Christ comes together in times of need to assert the Love of God in advancing the kingdom. You will have love and support around you, but it may not be the people you had hoped. Be prepared for some people to be offended, even assertive and mean-spirited. The ego-centric part of us that has played the game with other carnal-minded people will begin to battle for control. When this happens, it is extra challenging to not retaliate, but we must continue to focus inward on the transformation God has for us. No one and no thing is worth sacrificing the peace God offers. Although it may be extremely painful at times when God removes people from your life: LET THEM GO!!!! This is strength through humility, yielding to overcome, and surrendering our will fully to the One in Whom we can trust: Jesus.

HE CALLS THEM BY NAME

There comes a definitive point in the spiritual walk where we must decide just how deep and how far we are willing to go. Just how committed are we willing to be? Examining all this world has to offer, how much will we sacrifice in order to tangibly experience the absolute sovereignty of God and rest fully in His providential grace? Are we willing to be stripped of our wealth, titles, identities, roles, and accomplishments? Are we willing to be stripped bare and surrender everything we have worked for, deserve, and everything we love? No more wrestling. No more doubting. No more negotiating or bartering with God. Laying prostrate and with intense humility allowing ourselves to be emotionally, mentally, and even physically stripped down to bare bones, and from sheer exhaustion say, "Not my will but yours." How much are we willing to surrender to be given an all-new identity in Him and Him alone?

God wants to give you a new name, and it isn't Bitterness.
God wants to give you a new name, and it isn't Angst.
God wants you to give us a new name, and it isn't Rebuttal.
God wants to give you a new name, and it isn't Judge.

God wants to give you a new name:
Beloved, Holy, Bride, Friend, Righteousness of Christ, Salt of the Earth, New Creation, Anointed, Light of the World, Fearless, Strong, Redeemed, Free...... FORGIVEN!

TESTIMONY

This writing is as raw and bare as I can possibly be. It is dangerous and painful, scandalous and beautifully authentic. When talking about the subject of sexual assault, it is adamantly necessary to be as intently real as possible. If it is not spoken from the place of bare to the bone rupture, then it is not honest... it is not poignant, and it is not the whole truth. It is not fair to ask a victim to choose their words cautiously or minimally when describing the horrors endured. It is in fact an insult to expect a victim to soften the blow to spare someone else's offense with language. This is the whole truth about a child forced into daily sexual assault. A child without a voice who now has the opportunity to share, knowing that there are vast stories just like hers. This is her story, this is my story of suffering untold travesty and healing promised at the foot of the Cross and the Third Day. Be open, be aware, and be blessed. I so love the woman I have become.

I don't know exactly when the sexual assaults started. Best I can guess, around three years old. It isn't an easy thing to remember, much less deal with. I spent my whole life trying to forget how it felt, trying to not remember. It makes you numb to everything. I think I did fairly well in life considering I was involved in a full-blown incestuous relationship with a grown man when I was three to five years old. It is a suffering that only those who have experienced can understand.

Looking back, it all seems so fake. The birthday parties, the Christmases, the Sunday lunches after church. I suppose children living in the midst of the kind of suffering that comes with surviving trauma just try their best to piecemeal moments of joy or maybe some clarity into what it might feel like to just be a normal kid. But you don't really feel, you just shove all the feeling down to avoid that one thing: what if felt like to have someone force their hands and their body onto yours. Doesn't leave much room to enjoy ice cream or fishing. The only real consolation I had was an imaginary friend who became quite a comfort to me.

The entirety of my life, up until age 43 was spent wondering what I did to deserve it. Growing up in a time when children did not question adults, especially the good Christian adults, it was easier to just make it all my fault. Somehow accepting blame created this false sense of security that formed the belief, if I could figure out what I did to cause it, I could prevent it from ever happening again. It is so strange the logic of a child and how those core beliefs carry throughout adulthood. And how society, especially in the south at the time amplified this by suggesting young girls dress a certain way so as not to entice men. At about age 5, I remember wanting this pretty yellow and white dress that had an open back, like a halter top. My mother was hesitant but allowed me to have it. When we got home, she sewed a shawl to wear around my shoulders. I didn't understand. The shawl was awkward and uncomfortable and created conflict when I wanted to play. She explained that some men have a problem with bare backs and exposed shoulders. I suppose she was protecting me the only way she knew how. She too had been traumatized by sexual assault, only her perpetrators were two women. As an assault victim, this shamed me deeply. I was immediately aware that my 5-year-old body was a threat. That notion solidified the thing I had wondered all along. So, it actually was my fault?

I also remember distinctly wondering how I was dressed all the times I was assaulted. Were my shorts too short? Were my shoulders exposed? Was I asking for it somehow? I WAS THREE YEARS OLD WHEN THIS STARTED AND IT TOOK 40 YEARS FOR ME TO REALIZE IT WAS NOT MY FAULT.

I'm not sure where the breakdown of communication is in our culture, or what the deal is with hypersexuality.

How can anyone truly be sexually attracted to a child and why are we normalizing it? Why are we entertained with consuming assault, especially the assault of the helpless? What is the draw to the destruction of innocence? I am sure there are answers in the fields of psychology, but why can we not seem to stop it? Or at least address it with some clarity? And why is it now the norm? Why is sex so heavily marketed and why are we pretending it is not affecting our children and ultimately all of us?

I didn't really date in high school. It was challenging to bounce back and forth from wearing my older brother's oversized clothes to just covering up and wanting to dress like a girl. I didn't cheer because the skirts were too short, and I was worried I would tempt someone. I had a teacher proposition me once.

I was 16 years old and this man, who was our authority figure made a very clear proposition about having dreams about me. Again, self-analysis... what had I done? Were my shorts too short? Did I seem flirty? Should my t-shirt be larger to hide my breast? I was petrified and driven deeper into my shame.

I managed a fairly smooth adolescence, but one thing rose up and continued to rise. I was so deceitful. I knew this about myself and remember wondering if I could actually be different, or was I just this kind of person. I cheated on tests, stole money, stole clothing and makeup. I knew it was wrong but seemed unaffected by that knowing. I certainly do not remember feeling guilt at the time. When I was much older I did, of course. Once I had suffered the embarrassing consequences of theft, my eyes were open to the depth of that sin and my deceitful nature.

I may not have the education to speak well of the human psyche, but I clearly see the unraveling of my own story....my warped mind. I had been compromised at such a young age my mental state did not develop properly. I wanted to feel anything other than victimized, that seemed like such a weak position. So, to try and take authority over that vulnerability, I learned to play the game. Unfortunately, it's a game where no one wins. The game of fighting fire with fire ultimately led me down a path of hurting a lot of people, before my crash and burn.

As a kid, once you have a secret about an adult, you kind of hold all the cards... or so you think. Honestly, that is the poorly developed logic of a child. Once you learn that level of manipulation, there is an entire identity inside of you forming and taking root. When you have been told your whole young life to keep the secret, it is absolutely impossible to live without deceit. Your life is grounded in it, encamped around it and it manifests as identity. I did my best. I tried to tell a couple of people but no one believed me.

So, I shoved it on down and got tough. Thus, the game continued. Eventually, the memories faded from my surface awareness, re-emerging when I was 17 years old. Hard, hard reality even at that age. The flashbacks, the nightmares, the anger over not being able to confront him. This is when the real battle began.

I was sexually reserved through high school. Cautious at every turn. It was a different time back in the 80s in South Alabama. Raised up in the sweetest church, Christian Home, our whole church was family. Now I did a lot of things to disappoint my personal family and my church family, but being sexually promiscuous was not one of them. It scared me. I was cautious with that part of myself out of shame.

It was after marriage that I really began to explore my sexuality. It was in that committed relationship the allowance to discover that step of becoming a woman. But the wounds were still there, the scars so raw there is no way it would have ever worked. I was broken and too young to even know how to repair it. There were no easy resources back then, and it was still a big secret I was protecting. So funny we are as a culture that we actually protect the perpetrators. There is some weird kind of bond created so that the victims actually carry the weight of responsibility.... Yeah, even the 3-year-olds. And we carry it our whole lives unless we come to a place of awareness. Thank God, literally, thank God I came to that place.

I share this story because it is the story of so many men and women. I share this because someone out there still thinks it's their fault. We may try and use adult logic to filter the truth, "No way was it my fault, I was just a kid." But the core belief is there, the root identity is so deeply established that no adult logic can truly overcome it until you're able to see it for what it is...*the big lie.*

We all have a big lie somewhere in our lives. I have had the advantage of counselors and close friends who have helped me uncover all the lies and eventually the *big lie* was revealed. When we develop these core dysfunctional identities at such a young age, our lives actually manifest from those core beliefs. My core belief came out when I was 43 years old, and it shocked me. I had no idea and am deeply moved and grateful for the woman who held my hand and walked me through the darkest closets of my soul. Rose Phillips as guided by the Holy Spirit, literally saved my life. I sat in counseling with Rose weekly, sometimes twice a week for a solid year and then quite frequently another year. As my mind unraveled, so did I and so did everything around me. The most beautiful mess was made, and I found my redemption at the foot of The Cross.

So what was the *big lie*? Rose had me do an exercise where I wrote letters to all the people who had let me down and who had hurt me. I wrote letters to my parents, my ex-husband, to my current husband, to myself, and others. The last letter I wrote was to the perpetrator. Because I write well, the letter began quite diplomatically (still protecting him). But as I continued, it became more and more real. I got real honest, real fast, and once those closet doors opened, the darkness just flooded out. There were two pictures of me as a child 3-5 years of age laying on my nightstand. My exercise was to honor that child. When we are yanked out of childhood and forced into an adult world, we lose the ability to reconcile the lost innocence. I looked at those photos daily so I could be continually reminded that IT WAS NOT MY FAULT. That took a while to sink in, and releasing that lie was hard. It was so engrained. That was a lie that had carried me my whole life and helped me avoid recognizing my vulnerability. It was a major lie but not the BIG ONE.

As I wrote and wrote that letter, I wrote this statement and it floored me, it literally took my breath away, and I threw my notebook down.

Once this lie was exposed, it changed everything for me.

As writing the letter to the perpetrator, this statement emerged:

> *"I had one gift to share with my groom and*
> *you robbed me of that. I had one priceless*
> *attribute. You stole it and made it your*
> *own. No matter how I dress, no matter*
> *how I try to be and look my best, I can*
> *never cover you up or wash you away. No*
> *matter what I do I will always be a*
> *dirty, nasty, filthy little girl. You did*
> *that to me and it can never be undone."*

I remember how it felt coming out from under that lie. I threw my notebook down, looked at my childhood photos, and screamed out loud "My God...that isn't true!" "That absolutely is not true!" And I wept, and wept and wept until there was nothing left in me to leave.

This is where my journey with Christ really began. I was baptized on Easter Sunday 2009 by my brother Wesley. I was so free from that lie, and it felt so good to walk out of that grave. There was still some unraveling though. Yes, we may be made new in Christ, but surrender is a lifelong process of growing in intimacy with God.

When deep hurt happens at such a young age, the effects stunt our mental, emotional and spiritual growth, especially when there are no physical scars. When we have a physical injury we can look and say, "See what they did to me." But it isn't that easy with hidden assault. What do you say when you can't prove it? How would a 3-year-old describe a sexual assault? They don't even have the capacity to understand their bodies yet. And the worst part is the grooming. The perpetrator slowly lures you into an agreement.

There are gifts, treats, and gentle persuasion. And then the body itself has natural responses that should never be awakened in a child. How in the hell do you reconcile assault with pleasure? How do you reconcile pleasure with manipulation? Both are huge problems in our culture.

I have found it to be true in my life, only by growing in intimacy with Christ can all those wounds be restored. Funny thing about how He works. He doesn't just heal the wounds, he doesn't just set you free, he doesn't just create an all-new identity and restore your innocence. He somehow takes the worst of the pain, the vilest feelings, and raises them up to such a place of intimate love in him that he actually makes them HOLY. And you know what else I have learned? ONLY HE CAN DO THAT. He can give a HOLY purpose and a divine order to the worst of the worst. That's why the world condemned him and still does. He walked in direct rebellion to the carnal world and showed us the way OUT.

The one thing darkness cannot maneuver around or through is the love born of forgiveness. Now it would be a stretch to say that forgiveness comes easily, especially during the healing process. I have learned one thing about deep, intentional forgiveness; it is something the Holy Spirit does for you. It requires an honest commitment to wanting to be free and continuing to choose freedom through radical obedience. This is never something I could have done alone. I didn't want passive forgiveness, I didn't want logical forgiveness, I didn't want to cognitively separate myself from the pain and pretend I was free. No, I wanted to be totally free from the original exploitation and all the ramifications that followed it.

Now, people will give you all kinds of advice on how to do this. I even had someone once tell me that having a perversion toward my sexuality maybe something I'd have to accept. Honestly, I understood that and for a long time, I accepted that. BUT.... that is not what Jesus said. He does not want us to settle. He has the full capacity to bear the weight of us no matter what, and to set us free...ultimately meaning, to restore our innocence. I wanted everything I had been robbed of to be restored, and I knew Jesus could do that.

Because of his promises to me, I knew one day I would come to a place of full forgiveness, but for me, that has been messy business and unfortunately, has become messy for the people around me. There is no way to avoid that when in counseling. You go into it thinking you can process all this pain, disgust, and self-loathing with an adult mind and adult logic, but that isn't how it works; at least not for me. I had to walk through the trenches, dig into the pain and feel all that from the position of a child.

I had to address the violation, the breech in my innocence, from the place of innocence so it could be restored. This time, there was no place to tuck it in, no place to cover it up, and no place to hide. Some of the scariest days of my life, but I just hurt and let it hurt until there was no more hurt. I literally laid down on the floor a few times and tried my best to die, and when I did not die, I got up and lived another day. It was a two-year-long process of healing and still today, God shows me old habits, thoughts, and beliefs that do not align with his love for me. In His light, surrender becomes so peaceful.

For me, forgiveness has become a daily practice of surrendering and asking for wisdom. A couple of years ago, the Holy Spirit enlightened me with information that gave me a unique insight into my perpetrator's life. I had a dream and saw him as a little boy. He was in a barn, wearing overalls. I did not see the whole scenario, but he was crying. He was sexually assaulted by more than one person.

I woke up in a panic, and all I could do was weep. Some part of me felt compassion realizing, how deep the generational bondage runs with trauma. That was a huge step, but still not full forgiveness. Again, forgiveness is a part of healing. That is a whole being rescue, thus a continual process. The decision to forgive is a radical act of obedience, it is not usually a logical decision. Sometimes it can feel like saying that the violation is ok, but that is not at all true. Forgiveness is saying, "I will not repay to you what you have done to me, and I will not pay that forward."

Unforgiveness often leads us to make others pay for our suffering. Unfortunately, my inability to address and forgive the assault at an earlier age cost me and others. I hurt a lot of people trying to manage life from a place of brokenness. The closest intimate relationships suffer the most. Ultimately, we recognize this and forgive ourselves, knowing we have done the best we can. God takes it from there. Then we can ask those we have hurt to forgive us, which may or may not be allowed. It's ok... God takes over when we let go.

I share this brief synopsis so people can truly know me and know the answer Jesus offers. So those who have been traumatized as children can know, it was not your fault. So we can know and accept that there is hope for full restoration. So we can stop playing the game of "eye for an eye," and recognize that true healing takes place with forgiveness; the kind of forgiveness that requires radical obedience and the bold, courageous belief that you actually can be free. That freedom brought me to the solid realization that sex is either sacred and holy or it is not, but there is no middle ground.

Our culture would have us believe that you can mix that which is sacred and holy with manipulative, exploitive, and deceitful intent, but you can't. So, I decided for myself that sex and all things sexual are sacred and holy and good and righteous, and nothing in this world will ever compare to the meeting of two souls in that divine place. Don't think for one minute that you have to compromise, you don't. Believe me, you can find total freedom from the primitive world and all the false identities it hounds you to agree with. The carnal world leads in one direction: spiritual death. Don't fall for it, it is all a ***big fat lie.***

Working on this book with my older brother Todd has been the most painful yet beautiful process. This process has fulfilled in me the promise Jesus makes to take the worst of the lot and somehow make it all holy. He can do that for anyone, anytime.... you just have to ask and keep asking and not give up.

I am living, breathing proof of the fullness of His Grace.

-Much Love ...Kacy

QUESTIONS FOR CONTEMPLATION

1. Based on this study, WHY did the people that have hurt you do what they did?
2. What does Jesus say about why they did what they did?
3. How does Jesus see the people that have hurt you?
4. What keeps you from seeing them the way he sees them?
5. CAN you trust God enough to let Him have them and deal with them?
6. Can you pray for him to have mercy on them as he has mercy for you? WHY OR WHY NOT?

FORGIVEN

As day closes and night is fallen
Fatigue sets in and sleep is calling
For most it is a time sweet sweet rest
But alas for me its just another test

Eyes closed in hope of peaceful slumber
Rest and sleep I pray unencumbered
But just as he does every night
The enemy comes to me looking to fight

To the graveyard of the past I stand alone
I smell the stench of deadmans bones
Familiar graves all known to me
No matter where I look its all I see

Mistakes of the past ,doubts, and fears
All stacked up along a huge river of tears
One by one the graves open wide
The memories in a row now side by side

Things done to me and things Ive done
I look to the sky but there is no sun
And as they do each and every night
One by one they come into clear sight

I see the ones who betrayed me and lied

I feel all the beatings and I cringe inside
I see myself doing the exact same things
The people I hurt and I feel shame's sting

One by one they pass me by
I struggle for words but only can cry
They wrap around me like a fisherman's net
I read God forgives why cant I forget

I hear a gentle voice above all my cries
It says listen my Son lift up your eyes
The moment I do I am completely amazed
I see a bright light that locks in my gaze

I see a man hanging on pieces of wood
Head, hands ,and feet covered in blood
In a flash I was standing there at the base
Our eyes interlocked now face to face

The image is so horrid I quickly turn away
The moment I do I hear him say
Father forgive they know not what they do
The voice beside me says one word : TRUE

I stand and say I dont understand
These things are done by my very hand
And those that hurt me were in their
    right mind
When they were abusive and oh so unkind

Listen my son and I'll tell you why

All of you have bought into one big lie
The enemy's tricked all just like Eve
His only goal is to decieve

His goal is the destruction of relationship
All eat the fruit and into falsehood slip
Living a life of guilt and shame
Merely pawns in a Satanic game

But that not how its meant to be
The truth is what I want you to see
All in the world are loved by me
Its on full display up there on that tree

My only son went there for all mankind
So blind could see and sight would go blind
I want you to see yourself just as I do
Because in that alone is the real you

So trust in that cross and let me forgive
For in that alone is how I want you to live
Past mistakes well they are now mine
Forever erased from my Holy mind

And just as I have loved and forgiven you
You will now love and forgive too
So sleep now my son youve eneterd my rest
When tomorrow comes just do your best

And if by chance a mistake you make
Now and forever you're my namesake

That never changes eternity is set
I HAVE FORGIVEN DONT YOU EVER
     FORGET !!!!!

— TODD WHALEY, FEBRUARY
8, 2020

ABOUT THE AUTHOR

ABOUT TODD WHALEY

Todd Whaley has been a licensed massage therapist in Dothan, Alabama for over 17 years. He and his family own N-Balance Center for Structural Bodywork. He is a graduate of Troy University with a degree in business management. He was a lay minister for seven years.

Todd has taught The Four Gives of Forgiveness study in churches, community Bible studies, and prison ministries for over ten years. He has been married to his wife Tammy for over 35 years, they have one son, T.J.

ABOUT KACY WHALEY-GREEN

Kacy Whaley-Green is an entrepreneur and freelance writer. Being self-employed for over 25 years, she is the sole owner of The K Green Companies and operates K Green HAIRSPA in Dothan, AL. Aside  from ghostwriting, Kacy often participates in writing articles for local magazine Wiregrass Living, a Big Baine publication. Her history in the beauty industry has afforded her great insight into leadership, service, and ethics.

Her greatest love in life is family: her children Curtis and Saylar, along with a multitude of fur-babies, as well as extended family and friends. She is well known and appreciated for her ability to put pen to paper and spill out plain grace.

CPSIA information can be obtained
at www.ICGtesting.com
Printed in the USA
JSHW042146201222
35241JS00004B/17